MUDDY BOOTS
and
SUNDAY SUITS

To Joyce

Also by the same author

MUDDY BOOTS
and
SUNDAY SUITS

FRED ARCHER

ALAN SUTTON PUBLISHING LIMITED

First published in the United Kingdom in 1973
by Hodder & Stoughton Ltd

First published in this edition in the United Kingdom in 1992
Alan Sutton Publishing Ltd · Phoenix Mill · Far Thrupp · Stroud
Gloucestershire

First published in paperback in 1995

British Library Cataloguing in Publication Data

Archer, Fred
Muddy Boots and Sunday Suits. – New ed
I. Title
942.44092

ISBN 0-7509-0961-7

Typeset in 12/13pt Garamond.
Typesetting and origination by
Alan Sutton Publishing Limited.
Printed in Great Britain by
WBC Limited, Bridgend.

Contents

CONTENTS

CHAPTER ONE

The Light of Day

As the Worcestershire Regiment landed at Cape Tekke, Gallipoli, under heavy fire in the latter part of April 1915, John Masefield wrote: 'Many brave Worcesters went out to cut the barbed wire and were killed. Every man there earned The Cross that day.'

That week I was born near a fifteenth-century Cross at Ashton-under-Hill, Gloucestershire, bordering Worcestershire, in Stanley Farm House. It's a sobering thought to contrast the slaughter of total war on that Peninsula east of the Aegean Sea with what is commonly known as the accident of birth in a quiet village under Bredon Hill.

As my mother lay under the timbers of the sloped bedroom ceiling where the dormer window framed a picture of the church tower and the coppering beech tree, Uncle George hurried with Min, the pony, in the milk float to fetch the nurse from Beckford. He sat on a pot hamper, tugging the reins, with another hamper beside him as a seat for the nurse. 'Hurry, George,' Dad shouted from the back door as Uncle and the float clattered across the cobbled yard.

'No gentle trot to the station this day to catch the milk train,' Uncle George thought as he dropped the leather reins on Min's hind quarters together with a 'Come on, girl.' Three ha'pence for tuppence Min's shoes sounded on the narrow road between the growing hemlock and the spring-fresh hawthorn hedges. Tightening the reins from his hamper seat, Uncle steadied Min to a trot down Rabbit Lane where, from their holes in the sandy banks, rabbits of all sizes scurried in front of them.

The nurse, ready with her bag, stepped into the float after Uncle George had let down the tail-board and put both the hampers together towards the front. 'Hold tight, Miss, my brother Tom says it's urgent!' were the only words he spoke to her. 'Maybe,' she said, 'Your sister-in-law has had one before, I remember.' The journey ended with Uncle George looping Min's reins over a gate post in the cattle yard.

Nurse Handy tripped across the yard over the court stones to where my father was waiting with an open door. 'It's another boy, nurse,' Dad said. 'He couldn't wait.'

Up in the bedroom Ellen Baker had dealt with the emergency. 'No trouble, nurse,' she said. 'He just slipped into my two hands.' Mrs Hill, the charwoman, had plenty of hot water in the iron pots hanging from the hooks over the oven grate.

By trial and error womenfolk have a happy knack of finding out what milk suits a baby's stomach. 'Keep to the milk from one cow, Tom,' Ellen Baker told Dad. 'You are fortunate in having a herd to choose from. George Jinks reckons that Peasbrook, the strawberry roan Shorthorn, would fit the bill.'

Peasbrook became known by George as 'the babby's cow' – not that a seven-pound helpless bundle needed all of Peasbrook's milk, but George saw to it that the Gaffer had a little can of her milk twice a day.

And so I had arrived and Mother, lying near the dormer window, saw the rich pink apple blossom of the Lammas Hay Orchard turn paler as the bloom dropped and the leaves became as green as the grass beneath.

The copper beech leaves grew and became bronze in the spring sunshine. The cuckoos competed with each other in the oaks by the church tower. Jackdaws nested in the gargoyles. Starlings in the hollow apple trees kept up a continual din from dawn until dusk feeding their young and mocking every bird of the fields.

All was just as Thomas Hornblower Gill wrote in the nineteenth century:

> The glory of the Spring how sweet,
> The new-born life how glad;

What joy the happy earth to greet
In new bright raiment clad.

While cousin Tom fought for 'The Old Country' in Flanders, a black-hooded photographer from Evesham took a photograph of me, a pudding covered with silk and lace, at seven months old. Then cousin Charlie's life was ended by a sniper's bullet in Mesopotamia soon after my first birthday. An innocent child lay in the safety and security of home. Village boys were dying in the Great War. Memories played tricks with the best of us, but hearing as a three-year-old, the midnight call of Police Constable Smith as he stood in our front porch shouting 'Zeppelins. Lights out!' is vivid and real. Dark red curtains, the colour of a Hereford cow, were drawn over the bedroom window to keep the candles' glimmer indoors. Why Mr Smith came was a mystery to me, and so were Zeppelins.

As the war ended and I played in the pantry where the sacks of flour, ground at Sedgeberrow Mill, the chest of tea, bars of lard and flitches of bacon were stored, I thought that all these things were commonplace in every house — not just an insurance against the submarine threat.

Months later, Armistice Day. Some of the village lads who had left in khaki returned in hospital blue and came home for good.

As Driver Beesley came up the Station Road, Mother encouraged us to wave little Union Jacks from the living room window. Then a trooper, putteed and spurred, walked smartly past. How foreign these men looked compared to the cow-haired greased billycock-hatted men of the farm; now slouching with two buckets of milk yoked to their shoulders, or following the plough with a rolling gait like a drunken sailor. The straightness of the soldiers' backs put them head and shoulders above the workers of the field.

I pottered to the workshop where Grandad Westwood's carpenters' tools hung in neat rows against the beamed wall and watched him start to make a wheelbarrow for me.

Grandad had bright rosy cheeks above his pointed beard, and his eyes were bright china blue. Although he was slightly built I only stood just above knee-high to him in my pale green cotton knickers and blouse to match. I was still wearing sandal-type shoes with one strap and a button – my elder brother had graduated into lace-up boots.

Grandad was a meek and mild man. I don't ever remember his ever complaining of his health, saying he was 'middling'. He kept orange wine in a cask with a wooden tap in his workshop. I watched him for hours as he chiselled away at the handles of the wheelbarrow.

When I did wrong and Dad put me across his knee, smacking hard at the green cotton knickers, Grandad straightened his back as he said: 'Not too hard, Tom, they be very thin.' I suppose Grandad Westwood was the first man to take my part as he dried my tears with his red spotted handkerchief and gave me a humbug.

Then one morning my champion from the workshop was missing at breakfast. 'It's a cold on the chest,' Grandma said. Next morning he didn't come down the stairs, but a doctor, with his leather bag, called to see him. Sunday came and Grandma told us that Grandad had gone to live with Jesus and the Angels.

'But he won't be able to finish my barrow there,' I said.

'He's better there,' Mother said, 'he won't cough any more.'

The curtains were drawn as I passed the bedroom window on my way to Sunday School, and that afternoon Aunty Polly came from Beckford and Dad drove us over in the governess cart to stay a few days with her and Uncle Joe. That was the two of us boys, my baby sister stayed at home with Mother.

When we came back, I didn't go to the workshop again. I just didn't want to see how far Grandad had got with making the wheelbarrow. His chair stood empty with its red cushion. The wooden arms were worn slightly by the grip of his fingers and thumbs over the years.

I said my prayers each night in front of the oven grate at Grandma's knee. Grandma sat in a winged easy chair between the fire and the clock. She was stout, and she prompted me over the words 'Pity my simplicity'. In the evenings she wore a navy silk dress decorated with white lace and mother of pearl buttons on the sleeves. A golden locket hung on a thin chain around her neck. She opened the locket to show me a photograph of Grandad when he was young.

The soldiers were still returning from the trenches of France. Ten minutes after a train stopped at our little station, some son of Ashton often walked uprightly towards home. Then, as Grandma made the usual currant cake in an enamel dish and unhooked the boiling kettle from the pot-hooks over the fire, I used to go to Evesham with Tom and Mother and the baby in the governess cart. Ponto, who slept in a waggon in the cart shed, put the harness on the pony – a chestnut called Polly – and with the shining brasses and the smell of leather we snuggled down on the upholstered seats of the cart. Dad sat at the back by the door, the brown reins lying across a brass bracket on the front. At a click of Dad's tongue, Polly trotted down the Groaten, past the station and over the bridge to the main road. The war was over but German prisoners marched under escort over Sedgeberrow bank.

Polly walked up the bank and Dad said it would be a good thing to get the prisoners to move the hill away then we could trot all the way to Evesham. 'What are they going to do with the Kaiser?' was on people's lips then. 'Who is the Kaiser, Dad?' I asked. 'Is the fighting his fault?' No one answered and I wondered what it had all been about. But I remember I saw my cousin Charlie's medals in Aunty Lucy's front room and a big bronze sort of plaque. His photograph was on the table. He looked handsome. Charlie had fought and died for us.

The journey to Evesham took about half an hour. Then we arrived outside the King's Head where ragged boys of all ages were eager to hold the horse for threepence while we did the shopping. The rubber tyres of the governess cart jolted slightly over the cobbled bit of Evesham, between the High Street and the pavement. A place where markets were still held some days and horses and drays, driven by cloth-capped market gardeners, mingled with the more sophisticated governess carts loaded with ladies sheltered by trap umbrellas, cane whips sticking out from the mudguard holders.

As the days lengthened in 1919, most of the fellows were wearing khaki jackets and puttees above their boots instead of the usual leggings as they followed the plough or harrowed the wheat and preparations were made for the peace celebrations in Little Piece.

It was unusual for a boy of four to be out after dark in the village, but I was taken to see the huge bonfire and I picked up the rocket sticks as they landed on the field in Blacksmiths Lane. Aunty Lucy and Mrs Baker were not excited about the end of the war to end all wars. Their sons lay in the fields of France and Mesopotamia. Life for me was sheltered, even, tangible. For them it must have been bleak. Grandma would sigh as she sat in her wing chair, but she didn't give up her baking, tea making, stew-jarring rabbits and hares.

I took my turn in the iron bath those far away Friday nights when the great iron pots swung from the pot-hooks to heat the bath water – hard water softened by Hudson's soap powder. Water where the temperature was taken by Mother's bare elbow and where Mrs Hill, the char, puffed and blowed her onion breath into my face as she towelled me dry.

Then came a dreadful epidemic of flu when half the village were laid low. As we went down like nine-pins, Dad sent for Aunty Polly from Beckford. Aunt Polly was stout. All the Archers were. She reminded me, as I think back, of Mrs Wiggs of *The Cabbage Patch*. There was no need for her to wear that brooch on her blouse with the word 'Mother' on it. Her whole attitude was maternal, a comfortable body.

Aunt Polly took the train from Beckford station so that she could get a lift with cousin George on the dray from Ashton station as he brought the empty milk churns back to the farm.

George put a pot hamper for Aunty to sit on, but a prompt horse in the shafts leapt forward before she was seated and

Aunty Polly fell from the dray and broke her arm. But Aunty Lucy came with all the interesting news and good intentions. She brought the medicine up to where I lay with my brother under the beams. She organised Mrs Hill with the cleaning and the washing. Then, as we improved, she brought our two little mugs, one for my brother with the words 'For a good little boy' on it – mine read 'Think of me'.

As the flu passed and the last of the camphorated oil had oiled my chest, and the ipecacuanha wine had done its worst, men who had been ill and were 'on the box', the club or whatever, walked in a sort of slow dawdle up and down our village street taking the air. They wore their Sunday go-to-meeting shoes; they held one hand, flat knuckles down, on the small of their backs. The urgency of daily work was laid aside. There seemed to me to be a special way of walking when you were on the box. Those who were off work had to be in by six. Surely there was an art in all this, if only it was to prove to the able bodied that they had been 'very middling', as they said, and now they were feeling 'pretty middling'.

When a coal strike came Dad didn't seem at all worried as we had five tons of coal in the coal house. For the railways, it was different. They were the lifeline for passenger traffic and all the produce of the land.

One Sunday I came home from Sunday School as usual with Miss Carter. Bursting into the house I announced, 'The strike is going to end.' Dad said, 'Who said so?', and I replied, 'We've sung it at Sunday School. "Stand up for Jesus, the strike will not be long".'

Sunday evenings around the fire, after a few records on the phonograph, Dad sang 'Now the Day is Over' and soon we were in bed.

'Where did I come from Dad?' I asked one night.

'A long way away,' he said.

'Did you buy me?' I persisted.

'You cost me over a hundred pounds,' Dad said. 'You cost me more than the other two.'

In our rambling farm house where the only light was the

yellow flame of the oil lamp and where we each had our separate candles, a thunderstorm when the heavens opened and whole landscape was lit by the lightning, was both wonderful and frightening.

'What was the noise in the night?' I asked Mrs Hill as she blackleaded the grate one morning.

'Just a moving the furniture up yonder in the sky, I reckon,' she said.

Grandma said it was God speaking to us. Then I asked Dad and he said it was two clouds hitting each other in the sky and making a noise and sending big sparks of lightning down.

'See God's promise in the orchard,' Grandma said. 'That's the rainbow. That means He will never flood the world again.' Then she told me about Noah's Ark. I ran through the trees making the ewes and lambs scatter as I chased the rainbow when the rain had stopped. Bonnie and her foal were grazing the orchard. They just stood and stared. I was sure the rainbow was settled on the Hay plum tree near the hedge, but when I got there it was gone. I tried to catch the next one by the withies near the stream, but that went again.

Then Grandma died in her sleep in the blue room where Grandad had seen the blossoming apple trees from the window under the yew tree the previous April for the last time.

Again I was whisked away to Aunty Polly's at Brook Cottage with my brother. Here I saw for the first time a farm worker come home with a healthy appetite to his evening meal. Uncle Joe's plate, piled with potatoes, cabbage, fat bacon, flooded with gravy, was like a little pyramid on the damask tablecloth covering the living room table. We had had our tea when he came in from the harvest field. The look of contentment on his moon-shaped face as he wiped his moustache with the kerchief he took from under his belt never crossed the image of any Lord Mayor of London. Then the apple pie, the oceans of custard, the sighing and belching alone breaking the silence. 'Cup of cocoa, Joe?' Aunty said quietly as she took away the empty plates – well, nearly empty plates. All the bits of rind or apple left went straight into the pigwash barrel. 'No, Polly, I'll have a drop of zider,' Uncle said as he walked slippered across the garden.

He went past the pigsty to his hovel, or tool shed. Here a sixty-gallon barrel stood stilted on a wooden frame: a barrel with a wooden tap and a crock jug underneath. I followed Uncle and heard the amber liquid flow into his pint mug. 'Ah,' he said as he emptied the first pint, and the sweat ran down his weather-beaten face in rivulets. 'That's better, Fred bwoy,' and he took another pint into the house. He lit his pipe – a curious bent affair with a silver band – but first he cut the cake of plug tobacco and rubbed it with a sort of ritual in the palm of his left hand with the palm of his right. The smoke filled the living room. Aunty opened the door and went into the pantry. Here she took the Camp coffee bottle full of home-made herb beer and undid the string over the cork and poured me out a glass of what she called her 'pop'. It was several weeks old and it fizzed and frothed in the glass. It tasted good. I wish I had that recipe which had stood the test of time. I looked across at Uncle Joe's chair and saw that the cider mug was empty and his pipe lay on the table. The evening paper had slipped across the mat from his hands. His hands were now folded across his ample waistcoat. Its buttons and the top three buttons of his trousers were undone. Even the brass buckle of his leather belt lay on his lap, slack and shining like a horse's martingale. Uncle Joe was asleep.

I had never heard snoring before like Uncle Joe's. It's true Grandad had made noises by the fireside like a simmering saucepan, but Uncle Joe was different. Uncle Joe snored like a howling gale down our wide chimney at home when Dad said, on a winter's night, 'It's bad for those at sea.' He roared like a lion, enjoying every minute of his respite from his day in the sun pitching the sheaves of corn. He changed into a different key as Aunty Polly said, 'Oh Joe, you do make such a noise.' Then turning to me and my brother she said, 'Would you like another glass of pop and a piece of cake?' Aunty Polly's cake was rich and tasted nothing like the ones Grandma had made. Aunty Polly used chitterling fat from the pig killing.

CHAPTER TWO

I Start School

To potter after Fred Randalls in the cow yard, meet Shepherd Tidmarsh with Dad in the sheep pens or sit on the stable bench suited me; there was always something interesting going on. But, at five years old, I had my old grey jersey packed away for Saturday, the sailor suit for which I had been measured so many times by a Bengeworth seamstress had to be laid aside and off we went to Gloucester by train to buy clothes.

Dad was particular that the flannel knickers, as they were called, were big enough for me to bend and long enough so that the hem could come down for next year. Then the navy-blue blazer with an enormous EPS badge sewn on it which meant Evesham Preparatory School. A pair of lace-up black boots replaced by shoes and galoshes and with a fawn raincoat, which served as a mackintosh and over-coat, and navy cap with another great red badge, a satchel and pencil case, I was ready to join my brother on the eight-fifty train to Evesham.

Miss Cope walked us to the station and saw us on to the train and then walked with us to Miss Morris's school.

I remember burning my hands on the brass step inside the railway carriage as I grabbed where it was heated by the steam-pipe in an effort to haul myself into the compartment. The train was usually full but I did like to get into the compartment a lady teacher from Tewkesbury got out of because it smelt of nice perfume. I thought she must have been very rich.

It was difficult at first to have to take orders from someone other than Mother or Dad, but Miss Norledge, my first teacher who taught the infants in the music room, soon made me feel at home.

She must have been twenty, with black hair held in place with a celluloid slide at the back. This exposed the whole of her face and brow with her tidied dark eyebrows. Her skin of creamed parchment made me think she was a fairy princess.

It's a debatable point to fix an age when a small boy first becomes conscious that girls are different.

When Miss Norledge sat at my desk with her right arm around me, steering the pencil in my right hand as we first made pot-hooks together, I felt mothered in the best sense. Could it be the scent of the delicate powder on her glowing oval face, or was it the gentle guidance of her hand that made me determined to please her? The bunch of flowers I took her the next morning was frowned upon by the bigger boys.

You see, in a small prep. school for boys only, Miss Norledge contributed something very difficult to define. Miss Morris was older; a well-built woman, a bit tweedy; I suppose she was in her forties. She rode a sit-up-and-beg bike which stood all day in the cloakroom on wooden stands to keep the rubber tyres off the flagstones. She played the piano very well. The letters ATCL were on the brass plate near the entrance door. So parochial was life in 1920 that she detected a Gloucestershire accent in me – Evesham was Worcestershire, Ashton in those days was not.

Our little group of infants stood around Miss Norledge as we sang 'There is a Green Hill Far Away' in the music room.

Strict church, Miss Morris was, and every morning we said the Creed. Being a product of a Baptist Sunday School when the words came, 'I believe in the Holy Catholic church', I was silent, not knowing what Catholics believed in.

The reality of life for a five-year-old was frightening. We had been told far too much far too early of evil, of sin and temptation. The Devil and Hell haunted me sometimes as I firmly believed I was destined for The Pit. To run up the churchyard on a Sunday, not to stand at attention bare-headed when the hearses drawn by black horses passed by, was unforgiveable.

There was so much to enjoy in life that death was a mystery. I remember Dad's shallow black bowler hat, slightly green, his black suit with cloth-covered buttons which he only wore when a villager was buried after being wheeled down the road on the bier and me peering through drawn blinds. But life was good at school.

Dinner consisted of banana sandwiches, a bottle of Eiffel Tower lemonade in summer and a hot cup of cocoa at Izod's, the baker's, in winter.

When I was six years old, relatives came from away. When I say 'away' that means by train. Their cases came from the station on the milk dray and I slept with a cousin in the green room, a room which later became the bathroom. My cousin was about twenty-five.

After a couple of years in my single iron bed under the sloping roof in my brother's room, there was something elysian about sharing a bed with Helen. Sleep was complete abandon of the conscious world as the former dreaded dark hours flew by with my little fair-haired head deep in the hollow of her breasts.

Then the school holidays at Easter when the birds started nesting. With a strong cardboard box, which Dad's teeth had arrived in by post from the dentist with lots of cotton wool, I went bird-nesting. We tramped miles over pasture and plough land combing hedges, banks and ditches for eggs. I'd been shown by the village lads how to blow a bird's egg clean of its white and yolk by first of all making two small holes with pins. The collection grew, helped by older boys who could scale trees and walk across the fallen withies in Carrant brook for moor-hens' eggs.

Searching, searching; always listening to the birds; the peewits on the hill where the eggs are so like the native stone that it takes a keen eye to find their nests. Robbing nests was frowned upon. We only took one egg out of a nest and always we were looking for the rarity.

The many variants of buntings laid eggs so similar it was sometimes necessary to compare our finds with those of our school mates or other boys of the village.

Tired, I'd arrive at Aunty Polly's for that nectar from her beehive-like cottage – the cool herb beer. She would pour me a glass as she rested for a moment from her everlasting baking of cakes, boiling of pigs' jowls, chitterling and omelettes, the rendering of the lard from the pig killing to try and cope with the insatiable appetite of Uncle Joe. Another twenty-score pig lay in two flitches in the salting lead while Uncle was demolishing a miniature Bredon Hill of scratching pudding. As the pure fermented apple juice flooded down his throat it sent his Adam's apple up and down above the stud of his collarless shirt like the pressure gauge of the pump on the church organ.

But it was soon back to school again. Cherry Blossomed boots and Bay Rummed hair and the season ticket sewed firmly to the inside of my blazer.

I suppose that women ran my life as Mrs Hill polished my boots, Mother parted my hair and Miss Norledge started me first with pot-hooks, then the three Rs.

That winter, when they had begun ringing the five church bells for Christmas (they always started practising on Guy Fawkes' night) and Dad and his partner and Jack Hunting had carried hundreds of rabbits off Bredon Hill – rabbits caught in wires, ferreted rabbits, shot rabbits, all to be sold by Alan Harding on his stall under Evesham's Town clock – a letter came from the Black Country.

As I shot corks at the target on the pantry door Dad said, 'For goodness' sake be quiet tonight. Your Uncle Bill won't last over Christmas.'

'Not again,' I thought. 'And besides, doesn't he drink cider? We are told at Sunday School that only the perfect are fit for the Kingdom of Heaven.' I thought of the rich man and Lazarus. How he pleaded with Lazarus for water to cool his tongue in the lake of fire and brimstone. At times like these when I was very young I wished I had never been born. Born from where? Where did we come from? Where do we go?

It seemed that the perfection needed to enter that 'Happy Land Far Far Away' could never be attained by a mortal like me. How did these men I heard at evening service at Chapel attain the seemingly impossible degree of holiness?

The week before Christmas a black-edged envelope brought the letter to say Uncle Bill had 'passed away'.

Dad and Mother went by train to the funeral. An older cousin and Mrs Hill looked after us. I remember the chestnut pony and the governess cart driven by cousin George to the station! Dad's shallow black bowler, greener than ever, his black cloth covered-button suit. Mother's black gloves, black-edged handkerchief, her hat trimmed with purple and a great hat pin stuck through her greying hair. Even the kettle on the hob looked blacker than usual. Goodness, how sad.

Dad and Mother came back before Christmas. The mistletoe hung on the cart nail from a beam in the hall, or passage as we called it, ivy draped the pictures, holly glistened in the candlelight from the carving on top of the grandfather clock. In the dairy two cockerels hung head down spotting blood into a dish. The Christmas puddings had been made before Uncle Bill had died. Dad had fished them from the copper boiler with a toasting fork by the pudding strings.

Mrs Hill picked the feathers off the birds and prepared them for the oven. She took the breast feathers home to stuff pillows with.

Dad soon became cheerful again as the phonograph was lifted on to the mahogany table, the table where I sometimes lifted loose bits of veneer. The cylinder gave some sort of music. We even had carols. But that Christmas was a bit quieter because of Uncle Bill's death. It wasn't considered respectful to make merry too much on such occasions.

Annie, who taught me at Sunday School, was fond of me, but I didn't like her kissing me too much when I was six. Just occasionally Annie had fits, being an epileptic. Once she had one during lessons. I was frantic as she lay on the floor and the superintendent put a spoon in her mouth. Every Sunday afterwards I prayed, when we were supposed to be reciting the

Lord's Prayer, that Annie would not have a fit in Sunday School.

Then the moat froze over and the big boys made a slide from the churchyard wall to the end where the moor-hens would nest later on. As the large pond was lit with stable lanterns at night, Dad took us up there to see Percy Wigley and Ralph Cotton skate figures of eight on the ice. Boys and girls played hockey with a pebble and bent withy sticks. But soon it was back to school again.

The numbers starting in Miss Norledge's music room were increased after the holidays. I was moved across the stairs into a larger class taught by Miss Pennington. I cried for Miss Norledge. She was my teacher. She had held my hand at drawing and making numbers in chalk on my slate. Together we had done perfect pot-hooks and formed some letters in pencil. When I went to the little house up the garden marked WC and coming back could not reach the back buttons on my trousers she fastened the leather loops of the braces for me. Miss Norledge was my teacher I thought.

Miss Pennington proved an able teacher for us boys. Her discipline was strict, but she was kind. Poetry seemed to be her favourite subject. How the imagination is stirred by the poets. When we recited how Horatius kept the bridge in the brave days of old, the scene over the River Tiber was so real in the mind of a boy of seven.

The Battle of Blenheim – when we recited that it took me right home to where Ralph Pratt was ploughing Finches Piece as Southey rhymed.

> And often when I go to plough,
> The ploughshare turns them out.
> For many thousand men said he,
> Were slain in that great victory.

Skulls turned up by the plough, I thought, by Old Kaspar. Then my mind wandered to the straight furrows of Finches Piece where the only things I had seen our plough uncover were broken tea cups, clay pipes, buttons and links from broken plough-traces.

Arithmetic again was repetition until it sank into our memory. Until it came almost by instinct, at Miss Morris's. Long passages of the Bible were learnt by heart, mainly from Isaiah, he being the most eloquent of all the prophets. And so school time passed from nine o'clock till four.

About that time an epidemic of smallpox broke out and the local paper stated there was a case at Tewkesbury.

Now Dad was not keen on having us vaccinated as babies so, travelling on the train daily from near Tewkesbury, I was at risk. The doctor came one afternoon and the three pricks in the arm seemed nothing, but I had seen other boys with red-ribboned arms looking pretty sore a few days after the doctor's needle had injected the vaccine. When the pink lint had taken off the top of the scab several times when it was changed, the doctor dressed it with oiled silk and it healed. Meanwhile we of the red-armed brigade sat in Miss Morris's room while the rest played during break, and she read out the Test Match scores from the daily paper to us. Wireless for us was a year away.

Grandma had had smallpox as a child which had left two red marks on her neck. I remembered that as I looked up at the wall in the class room where Kitchener and Edward the Peacemaker hung in their frames over the fireplace. French windows opened on to the grass where the boys played football and tag.

Although prep. school was interesting, the adventures lay in the journey to and from school on the train. Also dinner time in the Market Place where we whipped our tops on the level tarmac, which gave some sort of relief – an outlet difficult to express. Men of the village had told me they had never bought their tops at a penny each from Mr Coombs but had had them made at Ashton by wheelwright Miles on his lathe. Dutchmen, we called the tall slim ones; boxers the squat fat ones.

There was something very satisfying for me in making a whip from a hazel-nut stick, notched to hold the pudding-string lash. The crack of the whip as the Dutchman spun on its metal pin, the sight of red and blue circles slowing down almost to a halt, and then whack again with the whip and hoping against hope that the whack was not too hard – that is, hard enough to break a shop window. This was just a mere shadow of the fun I had back home where the countryside was my playground. The hedges and farmyards provided my toys.

Class II at school paraded to church on saints' days, and on one sad occasion we stood bare-headed in Bridge Street as the black horses pulled a carriage bearing the body of a class-mate who had died.

CHAPTER THREE

The Back Place

Our living room was a sort of mixture of kitchen and sitting room. It was always known as The House. The cooking was done there on the black-leaded grate. All meals were served there except on Sundays when we either went into the little dining room, where the fire smoked for years because a sweep left his brush up the chimney, or into the drawing room which had been renovated. Beyond The House lay the Back Place. An L-shaped, blue-coloured stone-slabbed floor where the huge timbers flaked with whitewash. Mrs Hill spent her time here at the brown salt-glazed sink or at one of the two copper boilers. The sack of kibbled maize in the corner was usually good for a rat when Dad moved it for Rip, the Airdale cross fox terrier's, benefit. There was a churchy smell about the Back Place; musty, damp. The sway over the fireplace had two pot-hooks from which hung an iron pot almost like a gipsy cauldron. Mrs Hill, I imagined, was brewing some secret potion in that pot, but in fact it was often a ham, something too big to cook in The House. She prepared the vegetables out there, then carried them into The House for cooking. The two copper boilers side by side were stoked on Mondays with slack coal. One furnace, as we called it, was for the washing and next to it stood the dolly tub and a huge mangle. The other furnace was used for cooking small potatoes in their jackets for the pigs. When the wooden rounded lids were raised by Mrs Hill, she could be vaguely seen in a cloud of steam stirring the washing with a stick or lifting it into the dolly tub. The smell of Sunlight soap and wet flannel filled the Back Place.

I liked the steam from the boiling potatoes best. Little

bubbles burst on the surface of the water as it simmered over the brown-skinned, round and kidney-shaped tubers. When they were cooked and the fire in the furnace hole went low, Dad ladled them out into a half sixty-gallon cider barrel and mashed them with a wooden rammer such as Jack Hunting rammed the gate post firm with, only this was bigger at the end. I remember sharpening to a point a nut stick from the garden and prodding a whole potato and skinning it and then running to Mrs Hill for a pinch of salt, blowing on it until it was cool enough to cut in half with my knife, then enjoying the flavour of potato cooked for the pigs, but very tasty for me too.

In the inglenook, sides of bacon yellowed as they dried straight from the salting lead. Backbone chines from the last pig hung from hooks in the whitewashed rafters. In the corner to the left of the back door a plain corner cupboard was fixed with cart nails. This corner cupboard was too high for me to reach. In it lay the mysteries of treating ailing farm animals. Turpentine, linseed oil, Cataline, Stockholm tar, sweet nitre, green oils, white oils, raddle for marking sheep – Dad's medicine cupboard when carter, cowman or shepherd needed these things. Another shelf was packed with calf powders for white scour, ringworm ointment, udder salve, fresh liquor. Then there were the twitches to put on horses, marking irons for sheep and cattle and Pettifers Mixture – a tonic for most things.

A row of coat pegs in plain wood stuck out like half a ladder inside the door. Here hung the outdoor working clothes and on the one nearest the hall Dad's broad leather belt. Dad always wore a broad leather belt with a shiny brass buckle, but this was a spare one which he used to carry the wicker peck baskets up the ladders when he was fruit picking – and to tan my hide when necessary. This was the Back Place. Coldish in winter except near the fire, and cool in summer. Little Mrs Hill nipping around in her harden apron charring, as it was called. She smelt of onions and eucalyptus. She wore steel-rimmed spectacles. Her hands were rough, her face red. It was here she picked the fowls, dressed them, put the eggs into boxes. This was her headquarters. One thing Mrs Hill did every morning was to boil an iron pot of water which Fred Randalls fetched to wash out the milk churns and scald his milk buckets.

I liked Mr Randalls. He played his tin whistle to me in the cooling shed. Always hymns. He was strong Chapel. Sometimes he sang as he milked the cows. His greasy cap was pushed by his grey-haired head deep into each cow's flank as he sat on the three-legged stool, made by Jack Hunting, and the three-gallon bucket between his corded knees. The milk almost sang into the pail as well.

I see the Back Place as a little power-house of both the farm and house. I used to sit and listen to Dad, Mr Bailey, his partner and Mr Randalls as they looked so serious sitting round the fire some winter evenings when Mrs Hill had gone home.

They were waiting for a cow to calve in the Lidded Place – a sort of sick bay against the cow shed. Every so often they went across the yard with their hurricane lanterns to see how things were going. Then the shepherd would come for Dad or Mr Bailey to help him lamb a ewe, or Ralph to discuss the working of the land for the early peas.

As a child of seven it was always so plain to me that The Masters, as they were known, rarely gave orders to the three key men on the farm. The conversation struck me like this. 'Well, Ralph, do you think the duckfoot drags will rise enough mould for the Telegraph peas, or the Larworthy scuffle?' Ralph's eyebrows would rise as he answered, 'You be men as pays, but if I was you I ud keep the scuffle off the ploughing. It ull only bring the nasty wet clay on top. The ducksfoot ull make a clinking job with three osses abreast.' At least communication with workers was usual on our farm fifty years ago.

CHAPTER FOUR

While the Sun Shines

My holidays from prep. school were spent mainly with the men on the farm. Two jobs which overshadowed everything else in summer were strawberry picking and hay-making. Rows of Tardive de Leopold strawberries 242 yards long took a man more than a day to pick one row. Dark red wedge-shaped berries glistened in the snow-white pound punnets in the July sun.

All the time from early morning light Ralph was scissoring away with his two-horse mowing machine the tall grass in the meadows. As the dew dried in the sun the mower rattled louder and the pollen blew in little clouds of powder-like sand at the sea-side.

Ralph, who so often mowed 200 acres in a season, lived in a world of his own those summer mornings. No one bothered about him as long as the swath of the sweet-scented mixture of herbs fell behind the blade. I suppose some mornings he started the circle of the hay fields at three forty-five. He did tell me he once overslept and started at five o'clock without breakfast. But Ralph's mowing, however important, was just the first stage before the hay was home and dry in the rick.

Ralph was 'mechanised'. But I am wary about talking of mechanisation in farming. It all began so long ago. Where did it begin, or when did it begin? Steam power, water power, horse power or oxen power? Basically it is anything devised to replace the labour of hands and the sweat of brows.

In the Middle Dewrest, a field name that ties up with Dewrest Lane, the eighteenth-century predecessor of the main Cheltenham Road, grew a heavy crop of hay. The winter water-logging and the May sun grew cocksfoot grass which Ralph described as tough as thunk – the raw hide laces which joined the thrashing-machine belt.

After the mowing most farmers used a side rake to push the half-made hay in rows or walleys ready for the pitchers. Not so with Messrs Archer and Bailey. It's true they had a very old swath turner to turn the swaths; the tedding machine lay in the stinging nettles in Tythe Court Orchard next to a broken bull float.

'Unsafe to use without a guard on,' George told me. 'Lots of time,' he said, 'I've heard the iron spikes fly just above my head as they parted company with the rotating arms.'

So it was usual for Bill Spiers or George Earles to use Min or Tom in the horse-rakes and top the mown hay in rows.

Hay-making lasted from late June until well into September but a sense of urgency prevailed continually. As Mr Bailey picked up handfuls of the ready turned swaths and sniffed them and felt them to determine whether the hay was ready to carry, I saw that the grass, a mixture of herbage, the vetches and clover, meadowsweet and a parasite Ralph called rattle grass, had turned from green to a bluish tint withering in the sun.

'It's fit, you know, Tom,' Mr Bailey said, 'but by the time it's raked into walleys we shall have night here.'

The 1913 Sunbeam stood in the gateway, and Messrs A and B fixed the rake behind the car and Bert was keen to ride on the rake and tip the hay into walleys.

'Not too fast will ya, Master Archer, it's going to be a rough road.'

It worked. It had to. And in no time at all Bert had rowed up seven acres fit for the waggons. Uncle George and Mr Bailey and the shepherd tidied it up, raking the bunts, wisps or whatever folk call it, of hay off the headlands into the walleys.

As Dad hitched on to a waggon the 1917 Fordson tractor sent over here *en masse* by Henry Ford to help win the war, the shepherd was critical of paraffin fumes spoiling good fittle.

Mr Bailey laughed, as he always did when the work was getting done. Then his usual remark was, 'We shall need every bent next winter. A lot of mouths to feed.'

To me winter was further away than to him. The sun shone. The flies worried horses and men. So a 'Greens' hayloader, one of the few implements Messrs A and B bought new, was hitched by a chain to the back axle of the waggon. A pin on each of the hubs of the rear wheels slipped it into gear. The loader was an endless chain of rows of lath joined by cords, the hay being picked up from the walleys by a drum of sickle-shaped tines and thrown into the conveyer. Dad sat on the iron pan seat of the tractor and put on a pair of goggles edged with brown felt. He wore a cloth cap back to front. I had heard of Brooklands race track and felt that we were there.

But no, the Fordson was granshed into bottom gear and with 'Hold tight' from Mr Bailey, Uncle George and Jack Hunting waited on the waggon for the first of a stream of hay. It flowed up the loader and dropped on to the waggon like a pale green mattress. Mr Bailey followed behind with a pitch fork or shuppick picking up every stray wisp.

*   *   *

On my eighth anniversary of the journey from the cradle to the grave, my birthday present was a real football – a case ball we called it. As Les, Jack, Frank and I kicked it around the Church Close near the Monk's fish pond, known as the moat, we sweated the afternoon away, mostly taking penalties as Jack stood goalie between two withy sticks. Just doffing our caps for a few minutes as we leant against the churchyard wall and watched the Revd Margett's say the last well-known words over the box containing the body of Jim Huins, an old soldier who had fought in the Zulu war; the Union Jack on the coffin; the farm men who carried him all dressed in black; the tolling of the bell. This was my first experience of a funeral. After the sexton had filled in the grave we stalked up to the lonely flowers. Stalked so that our boots were silent on the spring grass, and I wondered, thinking that the man sleeping under the yews was nearly eighty years older than me, and we started the football again until tea-time. Tea in a tent made from a rick sheet by Dad, among the apple blossom in Lamas hay orchard. Jelly and blancmange.

It's difficult to express the joy, the satisfaction of a boy playing with simple things he has made himself. There is no comparison with the mass-produced tin and celluloid of the shops.

In an age when Woolworths had not reached Evesham, the only shops where we bought the raw materials for our toys were the Penny Bazaar and Mr Coombs'. Here, catapult elastic was sold by the yard, and if the hollow elder stick was not very effective, Mr Coombs' pea-shooters, at either a penny or a halfpenny each, were the answer. No, we didn't buy peas. The round variety known as Telegraph were good ammunition easy to come by each February when the two-hundredweight sacks stood on the headland of the pea field and George steered the drill up and down the rows. A sight to remember on those fine February days which often come at the beginning of the month.

To see the fresh harrowed ground steam as it dried in the weak rays of the sun when the harrows covered in the drilled peas. Here the biting east wind was welcome, if only to keep the drill wheels going round free from the clinging clay. The horses' breath came from their nostrils with the regularity of a steam jet from an engine. Telegraphs needed planting in February. There is a season and a time to every purpose under heaven. 'A time to be born, a time to die, a time to plant and a time to pluck up that which is planted.' So reads the old black book which has so often lain on the window sill beneath a pot of geraniums for years in the country cottage.

When the March winds blew clouds of dust up our village street a few years before the tar came to bind the road surfaces, crazes started. There would be a craze for tops when, from Piggy Lane to Shepherd Tidmarsh's cottage, village boys took advantage of the hour of light left after tea to whip tops up and down the street as the farm men scuffed tiredly home from work.

In those days there were about three cars in our village and the only goods traffic not horse-drawn was the DCL Yeast van on its way to Mr Clements, the baker, and the Brooke Bond Tea Trojan chain-drive van going to Mrs Cresswell's shop. Little did I think that now I'd be looking both ways twice before crossing the road.

But crazes lasted just a few weeks and then another one emerged to the playground of the lane and field. Our hoops were from the farmyard, not the town shops.

Seed drills and horseshoes often lay abandoned among the hemlock and nettles of the rick-yard when they wore out or got broken beyond repair. Here was our chance to get a hoop. The wheels, about eighteen inches in diameter, were made of half-inch round iron. The wooden spokes and hubs when they rotted away left us hoops better than the flimsy wooden ones of the shops.

To run after an iron hoop down the hill of the village street and race against Frank, Jack or Alf, was great fun. But we found that by taking a piece of iron and persuading Archie, the blacksmith, to turn the end into a hook on his anvil after heating it in the fire we had a hoop stick which made it easy to set the pace of the hoop rather than the hoop setting the pace for us.

Pop-guns, catapults and slings stayed with us throughout the year.

Slings were made with a piece of soft leather from an old glove, cut with a pocket knife to about twice the size of a match box, then stitched at both ends so that two lengths of binder twine could be threaded through. This seems primitive, but so armed I felt like another David about to slay Goliath. I found slings dangerous as we swung the pebble-loaded thing around our heads and released the one string. The target was rarely hit. David did better.

Pop-guns were harmless, innocent fun. At the back of our privy, or 'petty' as Dad called it, the elder bushes, or ellun, grew tall. A mass of white bloom in the summer with berries hanging like grapes in the autumn when the birds fed themselves fat for the coming winter and spoilt many a woman's washing on the Monday morning line as they fouled it after taking excess.

Elder sticks with the pith gouged out with my pocket knife and the poker made a pop-gun barrel. The nut bushes grew as they always grew by the path side to the privy. Here the arum lilies or cuckoo pint shot through the cold earth early in the spring. The plunger for the pop-gun I made, as generations before me had made them, from a fairly thick nut stick whittled down with the pen-knife until it was exactly like the inside of a bicycle pump with a similar handle. It had to fit the ellun barrel exactly to force air through. Ammunition lay close by. The pith from the bored-out elder stick rammed into the barrel; with practice the gun shot with a loud pop.

No one ever told me that to shoot at birds with a pebble from a catapult was cruel. It was the accepted thing to do, and why should I, at eight years old, question it. There was a code of conduct when bird-nesting that we only took one egg from a nest if we hadn't got that particular egg. Neither did we rob the nest of a sitting bird. The stalking of wild life has been the way man sustained his own life over the centuries. This maxim did not apply to me but was inherent in me. The satisfaction which came when first I was able to bring home a rabbit killed with my own catapult! I'll never forget a catapult made from a forked stick, the elastic from Mr Coombs' shop bound on by thread from Mother's work-box. Again the leather which held the stone was just made from an old glove. We had that rabbit for dinner and I was proud that it had been killed by my catty.

It seemed a pity to me that with all the material around me for simple country pursuits, it had to be spoiled by school in the week and Chapel on Sundays.

Jack Hunting, one of the most honest men it was my privilege to ever know, and certainly the most ingenious, made on his carpenter's bench in the barn near the Cross, things of which I have never seen the like. He could mend anything in wood. He worked for Dad and Mr Bailey as their rough carpenter. In the evenings he made what he called 'fakeums', rat traps from bent saplings and the rabbit wire. Setting pins from broken spade stales. He made me a tip-cat. A simple toy, just a nut stick about six inches long pointed at both ends by his draw shave in his vice. This was essentially a toy for the level road. Placing it flat on the road the two ends were about an inch from the ground. Just a smart tap with another stick about eighteen inches long made the tip-cat jump vertically in front of me and with practice a swipe with the stick sent the missile flying through the air fifty yards or more. Tip-cat was great fun, but not too near windows.

On summer days at Holcombe Nap, where the grass was slick and wiry, the village children climbed that steep slope near the primrose coppice dragging sledges. Sledges in summer, you may wonder, but these sledges, made from the staves of cider barrels, careered down at a cracking pace on the slippery grass of the Nap.

The Nap belonged to Mr Clements and it seems likely that his family thought out the idea of summer sledging. I never really took part in this sport but was satisfied to go up there with my brother Tom to see a good many of the village youths enjoying this free sport which, to me, looked priceless.

Up alongside Holcombe Nap was the primrose coppice where the flowers grew under the shade of ash poles which grew on stools, or 'stowls' as the locals called them. These ash trees which grew in the coppice were lopped about every seven years to provide fencing materials, stakes and rails and were also used for hurdle-making.

The bigger boys of the village searched the coppice for home-made stilts. This searching had been a trait inherited from their fathers. The art of finding suitable poles for stilts was inborn. Like their fathers' when they looked for a scythe-handle or sned. The required stilt depended for its length, of course, on the height of the boy. The step to stand on was formed by lopping off an offshooting branch which grew as near as at right angles to the main pole as possible. Lopping off, that is, to leave a stump big enough to stand on.

I didn't venture on stilts until I was older, but it was a sight, an unforgettable sight, to see a dozen village lads walking hedge-high down our village streets on a spring or summer evening. Of course, some fell off while learning, but later they raced each other from Cotton's Lane to the village Cross. Whoever said, 'The best things in life are free' was so right in this instance. Oh you could buy gaudy painted stilts in the town shops with the foot rests screwed on to a straight stick, but these were 'boughten', as the old folk said, and boughten cake was frowned upon.

The sound of a cricket ball on a willow bat has been heard in the village for centuries. The village team used bats with pliable handles spliced into the willow blade. Handles covered with yards and yards of thread and often a rubber jacket over that. We made our own willow bats for cricket on the short cropped grass of the footpath to Paris across Church Close.

It would be truer to say that the bigger boys made them. They climbed the willows before they were pollarded and cut with a hatchet a sizeable pole, then split it in half with wooden wedges hammered in with an old gate hook. The laborious task then began. After the required length of split willow came the whittling away at one end to form a handle. It took lots of patience and changes of rough carpenters and pocket knives to create a bat. Bats made in that way would drive a ball but when we used the hard composition cricket ball from the bazaar, sometimes it stung the hands when a fast ball was bowled at the rick peg wickets. Wickets were no problem at all; bundles of rick pegs lay about the farm and they were ideal.

And so with hide-and-seek in the hay tallet, or loft, over the stable, Saturday morning paper-chases or fox and hounds over Bredon Hill, boys and girls had little to desire in the way of simple sport. A 'Do-It-Yourself' project, when even the slide down the straw rick cost nothing. Yes, the good life.

CHAPTER FIVE

Where Did I Come From?

It's reasonable that a boy of eight years should be inquisitive as to his origin. Dad's story that I cost one hundred pounds no longer seemed feasible.

Flocks of lambs cried like babies in the orchard every spring. I didn't know why cows had calves and mares had foals. No one seemed to be surprised.

We kept a bull – a Hereford with a white face and a red coat like moleskin. He was chained up to a manger. I had never seen him let loose. The cows' ties in the cow shed were dull chains with a wooden block or chog at the bottom. The chain moved up and down through the manger ring as the cow pulled the hay from the hay rack. I noticed the bull's chain was different. It shone like silver due to being continually slung around his neck. A leather washer was fixed between the T-piece of the chain and the round ring it was fastened to.

'Bulls must not be allowed to get loose, they are sometimes savage,' Dad said.

'Why are they savage and anyway, why do you keep him? He gives no milk and even in the summer time Mr Randalls has to give him hay.'

'Oh, sometimes we turn him out into the yard. It's company for the cows and they milk better,' Dad said.

One day during the school holidays, Frank and I were climbing the beams above the bull pen looking for sparrows' nests in a little loft with a slatted floor where some of Mr Bailey's fowls roosted.

A sound of 'Coop, coop, coop' came from the nearby road and Mr Baldwyn from the Croft was driving two cows with Bill Allen walking lamely in front.

At the entrance to the bull yard were a pair of gates fastened shut by an asp and staple and an iron pin. Bill flung one gate open and the two cows entered the yard. One was agitated and was riding piggy-back on the other one, leaving the dirty marks of its hooves on the other cow's flanks.

'Quiet,' I said to Frank, and we hid in the little tallet. The bull bawled loudly, more of a bellow than a bawl. His chain rattled as he hung back pulling at the manger. We waited and watched.

'Steady, now, Willum,' Mr Randalls the cowman said as he stroked the bull carefully until his hand reached the steel chain. He then undid the tie and Willum trotted into the open yard.

He made a circuit of the yard with his tail erect apparently ignoring the two strange cows. Then he sniffed the air with open nostrils and showing a row of white teeth. He pawed the straw litter in the yard with his two fore-feet, then tossed some loose straw about with his horns. Bill Allen then said, 'Come on now, we ant got all day,' and drove him with the ash plant he carried towards the cow in season.

After a preliminary little run up one side of the cow and then the other while she turned her head around, standing stock still, Willum sniffed again, feinted to jump on her back, looked around at the three men and mounted the cow.

We saw them couple. It lasted but seconds. Then we heard Bill say, 'Let him have another go just to make certain.'

'Make certain?' Frank said in a whisper. And we were puzzled.

As we slid off the beams from the tallet Mr Randalls had tied the bull up again but Bill Allen saw us, and pointing his stick at me said, 'I'll acquaint thee fayther. You yunt supposed to be yer.' And so for days I lived in fear lest Dad would find out.

One Sunday afternoon in the October sunshine, Frank and I

walked the footpath at the top of Clay Furlong. I'd seen Shepherd Tidmarsh put red paste or raddle on the brisket of the rams in the nag stable before they were turned out. One ram was with fifty ewes in Clay Furlong. He nosed them out like a dog scenting rabbits. Frank and I hid among the pampas grass in the dry ditch. He was busy mating one or another of the ewes. They were almost queueing up for him. Takes longer, I thought, as he was mounted in a more leisurely fashion than the bull. Every one he marked red from the raddled waistcoat-looking brisket. That's what causes the ewes to lamb in the spring. And we talked about it at school in the playground. The mystery of birth had been solved for me as regards the animal kingdom.

Jimmy, a friend of mine whose father farmed near Pershore, told me that every time a boar grunted when he serves a sow that means another little piglet later on.

Miss Morris said that a bullock was a young bull but Jimmy assured her that it was a castrated bull-calf. He had seen it done.

At Sunday School Mr Cotton, who had been a shepherd, told us of the Good Shepherd, and of how we had erred and strayed like lost sheep and needed to return to the fold. He was a kindly superintendent and often said, 'I wonder what you boys will grow up to be.'

Sunday nights at Chapel the theme was as ever that 'Here we have no continuing city but seek one to come'. The story of Adam and Eve was so instilled in my mind that I pictured the Garden of Eden in Carrants Field just across the railway level crossing. It was so positive in my mind that Eve gave Adam a Worcester Pearmain apple off one of our trees near the tool shed and that the serpent or snake lived in the swamp or withy bed by the railway bridge. If only Adam had refused the apple we would not have been born sinners, as I was so often told. We must have descended from old Adam, I thought, because all talk of our coming from monkeys originated from that evil spirit Satan, we were told.

That spring as I watched Shepherd Tidmarsh, one of

nature's gentlemen, deliver a lamb from a ewe in the Cross
Barn as I peeped through a chink in the weather boarding, I
knew that autumn mating caused spring lambing.

Then the ewe circled the little hurdled pen again, licked her
new-born lamb, flinched in pain and, lying down again,
heaved and grunted. Then two more feet came out from under
her tail and the shepherd knelt down on one corduroyed knee,
pulling gently every time she strained, until the head of the
lamb emerged. And what a relief as she dropped her burden. A
burden of five months' carrying. Do women suffer? I thought.
They must do. I came that way. But just because Adam ate
that Worcester Pearmain, why should I be born a sinner? It's
most unfair, yet everyone says it is so. But when we found the
sitting hen among the nettles and watched until her eggs
hatched out and saw the farmyard cockerels treading the hens,
the miracle of birth became plainer. How often, when one or
two chicks have been late leaving their cocoon-like shell with
the little beak and head stuck out all wet and slimy, I have
helped nature by removing the shell and in minutes the dry
chick has followed the broody hen across the rick-yard.

It seemed to me then that nature had a way which, to say
the least, was unfair. Lambs were born perfect. Calves and
chicks perfect. We, who were on a higher plane than the
animals, were born with a stigma.

At that time I was quite content with the Garden of Eden
story as man's beginning and that Eve was made from Adam's
rib, and now I knew that our entry into the world was much
the same as that of the lambs, the calves and the foals. But
why, oh why, I thought, do we have to start life with a
handicap? God created the world perfect. Everything perfect.
Why pick on us? Surely He is a just God?

Still at prep. school at least I knew the cause of our
existence. But what a nightmare it had been. Queen Victoria
had been dead twenty-five years, but the relationship between
man and woman was never talked about in the presence of the
young.

CHAPTER SIX

Where Am I Going?

Seventy years as the allotted span of life on earth seems an eternity when one has only had three years at school.

Seventy years, I thought, that's seven times as long as the life of Grannie, the oldest cow in the herd.

Miss Morris talked of a better land, Heaven, where all was fine. I rather looked forward to the idea of a place where there would no night, no colds, no pain, no aches. Ah, Paradise! Mr Cotton at Sunday School told us that no believer in God should have a 'fiddle face'. How true that was. But how soon I was disillusioned.

Chapel at night was different. It seemed to me as the preachers ground out the same story about 'two men being in the field, one shall be taken the other left', that I would be left. Thoughts came to my mind of a split family. When the fire and brimstone of Hell was preached with such conviction by venerable-looking old men, the fact that I would end up in that pit around the fire which could not be quenched was my conclusion. The times I have heard the warning, 'If you pass that door unrepentant, unsaved, turning your back on God's offer of mercy and conversion it may be your last chance. We are not promised tomorrow', the preacher said. 'Do you want, when this short life is over, to end up in a Christless grave? A lost eternity?'

My guilt complex then was worse than anything Hell could offer. Just to feel that a certain few were to enjoy the pleasures of everlasting bliss while I and millions more would suffer the torments of Hell.

Was that the way to make young believers? I didn't think so. Converts gained by the doctrine of fear. Fear for oneself.

Fear of something which is beyond the imagination. Eternity just didn't make sense. Surely, I thought, God is not like that. No, not like some supreme Lord Chief Justice looking down all the time for every fault, every error in me. I read my Bible and in stories like the Prodigal Son, the Good Samaritan, the Widow's Mite and the Woman at the Well, I read of a forgiving God. A God of love.

Where the doctrine of eternal torment for everyone except the chosen few who believed the Bible literally from cover to cover came in I never knew. This was Puritanism. Exclusiveness.

Oh the damage that can result in a Church ruled by fear. It can never be assessed. The blight which ruined the blossom of a young mind and spirit; stunted the fruits eager to emerge.

I took no delight in the story of the dogs licking up the blood of Jezebel. Nor of the farmer who built his barns bigger and died in the night. And so when the Salvation Army came some Sundays their band and male-voice choir brought with them a hope for the masses – even boys like me – which was sadly lacking in the Weary Willies who prayed for the Kingdom, and made it clear that the more we suffered down here the better it would be for us in the Land they were going to. I liked the attitude of the Salvation Army. A note of triumph over all life's difficulties without the 'thou shalt not or else' doctrines.

Forty-eight years ago it was dangerous in most circles to question the existence of God. I accepted that; but what puzzled me was how an ordinary country boy born in a small village in a small island on the map should have to go to such lengths to be saved from eternal damnation.

The folk in the established Church, although no one will deny that corruption has been all too present there just the same way as in other denominations, had a more positive approach than we had in Chapel. The set ritual and ceremony was finely worded and free from the threat of The Pit. It is true that the emphasis on the sacraments was greater. There was a code of behaviour. But I was too young to question who knew the truth.

The fact of Jesus Christ's life on earth is an historical fact.

If a person believes that He was God's son, that is an act of faith. Man being born with a spiritual appetite means that he must believe in something.

So man believed in God. Oh yes, it was drummed into me how wicked the uncivilised, mostly coloured, people of the world were with their witch doctors and superstitions. How could they believe in such things? The missionaries had been working, and let me say here, doing a great job medically but, and here lies the crunch, they destroyed native culture to replace it by the doctrine of the Nazarene.

It's true His life was a good life; His doctrine that of love. It is also true that the simple message He brought, a wonderful message as recorded in the Bible, has been twisted and manipulated to man's own advantage.

Paul's interpretation of what Christ stood for was to suit himself. This version stayed with me as a chain around a cart wheel – a brake – and gave me a loneliness which is hard to describe.

And so, feeling alone at such an early age, the message that God was a God of love and that He could be seen only through the people who practised going the extra mile appealed to me. This message was first explained to me when Mr Gilbert Roberts, of the Caravan Mission to Village Children, came with *Good News* to Mr Nicklin's orchard.

So the fable that the Almighty had the machinery of torment for the punishment of all who failed to conform to man-made rules was out. To think that folk even imagined it feasible that millions would spend eternity in a lake of fire! If that was true I didn't want to be one of the so-called Elect. No, much better, I thought, even to be with the verminous tramps who slept on our farm, who picked peas by day and drank at the weekends.

George Fox had said, 'There is that of good in every man.'

No one can prove the existence of God or eternal life. Neither can anyone prove it to be false.

I called this chapter 'Where am I going?' I think this is a question which applies to the whole world. And any of us who try, during our short life, to make that life a little easier, a little happier for just a few with whom we come in contact, can create a little heaven here and now.

CHAPTER SEVEN

Strawberries for Tea

When strawberries were picked and punneted in one-pound square chips and six-pound baskets, it was often that fruit we had for tea after we had walked the station road from school. Our satchel-swinging group lazily made its way past the hemlock, cornflowers and marsh mallow of the roadside verge. Drays drawn by trotting nags queued at the station yard while Mr Boucher, porter in charge, directed them to the waiting railway trucks for towns north and west.

The dust, the hot sun on the still untarred road, was choking as they passed and Stodge, the roadman, shovelled the horse muck into the growing barrow of soil and road sweepings on the ditch side of the road.

I had swigged the ice cold water from the station pump and then remembered that my sister Clarice had invited some of her friends to tea. Clarice went to a little private school kept by Miss Kimpton at a house where the sundial told the time of day above the porch. 'Girls,' I thought. 'But there will be one of Mother's special trifles, ice-cold from the pantry crock and strawberries, then games.'

The oven grate in the living room, or 'house', made that too hot to eat in on a sultry July afternoon. The fire had to be kept going throughout the summer to boil the kettle, the saucepans and for oven baking. Despite the stone-slabbed uneven floor where the tilting slabs cut through the lino, the living room was uncomfortable in high summer.

Out in the hall, where it widened under the bay window, a square scrubbed table lay under a dark green tasselled tablecloth. Dad used this table every Friday night when he paid the men through the window.

Mother had laid the tea by the time I arrived home dusty from the train, and I wearily hung my blazer and canvas satchel on a wooden peg in the Black House.

Yes, tea was laid in the hall. The cool breeze wafted through the open front door and made its way across to the open bay window.

And so, with chairs from the living room, I sat on that summer afternoon with Clarice and Eileen, Marion and Jean and Ken and Dick who were both younger than me. After the refreshing tea we played cricket in the rick-yard, then Ken and I watched the farm men unloading the meadow hay from Didcot Ham.

The monkey pole was up alongside the rick. Dad stuck the great forks like grappling irons into the hay on the waggon. Shepherd Tidmarsh was building the rick with Mr Randalls while Bert led the horse to and fro pulling the cable which lifted the loaded forks towards the gib on the crane-like contraption.

'A bit more pudding,' Dad called to Bert as he wrestled with the tight rope. Bert backed Captain another yard and allowed the unloader enough slack rope to drive the forks into the hay with all the weight of his body taken up with Dad's strong arms and his one knee.

The horse moved forward.

'Hold tight,' called Bert and another forkful of fodder swung on the gib to Mr Randalls and the shepherd.

'Let go the painter,' they shouted, and Dad pulled the trip cord attached to the forks and the hay fell just where it was wanted on the rick. Every time a load went up on the rick the waggon emptied more and more until the shepherd, leaning over the side of the rick, chuckled as he said, 'Oi, I can see his bones.' The 'bones' were the raves, or sideboards of the waggon. The criss-cross marks of braces on sweated flannel shirt showed plainly on all the men. The brims of their straw hats were full of hay seeds. Every now and again they pulled handkerchiefs from under their broad belts and mopped. Mopped the sweat from their rosy faces. Mopped the hay seeds from under the neck bands of their shirts. Dick and I stood and wondered. Wondered how Shepherd Tidmarsh kept the rick so square at the corners, and I noticed the track of Captain which looked like a well-worn footpath among the goosegrass and nettles of the rickyard.

The men went home after that load. Then we climbed the pole and up on to the rick. Clarice slid down a loose rope, the one which held the forks. The friction of skin and rope gave her a burnt hand. She learnt after that to go down hand over hand when sliding down ropes.

'Let's play hide-and-seek,' Dick said as the bats swooped low in front of the stable door and Bert, after ungearing Captain, was taking him to the fields.

'Yes. Bags not to be on,' everyone shouted, and first Ken then Eileen closed their eyes at the den, which was the elevating pole.

The summer sun sank over Bredon Hill, the stable was dim inside but outside the air was cooler and the yellow pole of the den easy to find. We all got caught in turn as we came to the den like young rabbits from different burrows. Pigsties, lofts, behind the elder bushes – these were the usual places where village children played hide-and-seek.

'Come on, Marion,' I said. 'I know just the place.' And together we climbed a little ladder over the bull pen to a little tallet, or loft, which was divided for a fowl roost.

'In the corner, quick,' Marion said. And in the gloom we hid above the cud-chewing bull.

Marion put her chubby arms around my neck. Her frock was blue, patterned with white flowers. Her short sleeves were hemmed with lace. She had a round celluloid slide in her fair short hair. I kissed her on the cheek. She told me she loved me and asked me to marry her one day.

'One day,' I thought, 'and I'm only eight.' She told me some Indian princes had been in the village at the cricket match. One was nine and he was married.

'My den, one, two, three,' the others shouted. But Marion and I had those few precious minutes and when she kissed me again and again I felt that at last I was a young man and that I'd soon be building ricks like Shepherd Tidmarsh.

'Where were you when we called?' Ken and Dick asked.

'Never heard you,' we answered as we came down the ladder.

'Come on in now,' Mother called from the court by the back door. 'I've got some pop for you before you go.'

'Like Aunty Polly's?' I asked.

'Well, it's her recipe,' Mother answered. And, in the cool hall, we drank cool ginger beer as the corks fizzed and the pop frothed.

Dad lay back in the wing chair in the living room by an open window. The *Echo* had fallen from his tired hands. Rip, the dog, rested his head on his slippered feet. I thought as he sat there with his belt unbuckled and slung across his knees with little heaps of hay seeds which had fallen from his trouser turn-ups on to the yellow patterned lino, 'Dad's a wonderful man.' And I looked at his sun-burnt arms and saw how white they were just above the turned-up sleeves of his flannel shirt.

That night I dreamed of Marion and the next day I asked Jack Hunting to make her a trough for her pet rabbit. When it was finished I took it round to her house.

At the age of nine I moved into the top class at Miss Morris's. Some girls travelled by train but Marion still went to the little private school in the village. A pity really, because when I next met her in the village I was shy.

CHAPTER EIGHT

A Rabbit-pie Supper

Five years after the Great War was over the new chapel was shoulder-high with bricks from the old chapel. Services were held in the new Recreation Room.

That year, as Christmas drew near, the cattle were in the yards and the ewes grew big-bellied on the hill as Shepherd Tidmarsh filled the feeding troughs with his kibbled cake, oats and locust beans. Then he shook the sweet-smelling sainfoin hay into the wooden racks. Racks whittled from brookside withy by Jack Hunting.

'Less than two months to lambing time,' he told Mr Bailey and Dad as I followed them on one of their many excursions up Bredon Hill.

It seemed as if it was well nigh impossible to get away from sprouts. We walked that Saturday morning up and down the endless rows where the bottom leaves had been stripped by the pickers as they pushed the green buttons off the stems.

'Won't get your legs wet today, Fred boy,' Mr Bailey said as he carried his loaded twelve bore. I trailed behind the partners. Dad carried his gun on his shoulder and Mr Bailey's seemed to form a third arm as he held it at the ready. His left hand held the breech and the two barrels lay across his left arm pointing towards the next row of sprouts. Unorthodox perhaps. But they were unorthodox men.

'Ah, postcards,' Mr Bailey whispered to me as he pointed to where a covey of partridges had left their nightly droppings.

Laddie his dog got excited and both men pulled back the hammers of their guns and walked slowly forward about fifteen rows of sprouts apart ready for the rising birds. A hurried flutter of outstretched feathered wings buffeting the leaves on top of the sprout stems and the covey rose and flew away from us. A line of eight in full flight.

I suppose the action of man and gun co-ordinated in an involuntary way. Bang-bang, reported the right cylinder barrel as outside left and outside right fell dead among the sprouts. The centre of the covey was rising higher as Mr Bailey fired his left-hand choked barrel at a marked bird at three times the length of a cricket pitch. He shot to get the partridge in the head as it rose. Then came the all familiar sight as the bird, stunned and unbalanced by the shot, towered. It towered straight up in the air as high as Evesham Bell Tower, then like a stone it fell in front of us to join the other two among the sprout rows. Dead.

I put the three birds in a bag and we climbed higher up Bredon to shoot rabbits. The grass on Spring Hill was grey with the winter wind. The outlying heifers had grazed the green patches bare but left the December wiry grass as long as the June mowing grass. Here lay the rabbits and the hares. The cold wind had blown everything dry.

So we walked Spring Hill with Laddie at Mr Bailey's heels. Guns thirty yards apart and me like a centre-forward in a football team was how the field was drawn for the powder-puff-tailed so-nice-to-eat animals, said to have been brought to this island by the Romans. Bang-bang, as first one rabbit then another somersaulted in front of the guns. I carried the bag until it got too heavy, then Mr Bailey slung it up into an ellun or elderberry bush to be picked up as we came back. Somewhere from his pocket Dad gave me another bag with 'Carter's tested seeds' written on it.

'Put the next lot in there,' he said. 'We are going to Furze Hill.'

Over the brow of this hill I saw what looked very much like a pig-run. All the grass had gone and the fox-earthy soil was dug into mounds and holes went deep into the underlying limestone.

'Ought to get a couple apiece here, Tom,' Mr Bailey said as we stalked the brow and looked over the wall.

Just four shots on a part of the hill where the very earth seemed to move with rabbits sitting at the mouths of their burrows in one of the biggest rabbit holts or warrens on Bredon. I picked up eight rabbits as they kicked their last from the lead of four cartridges. Underground, the thumping of the multitude was a protest, a warning to stay in the earths.

We walked down the hill as the five-twenty train steamed out of our station. The Saturday train on which the peck-basketed men and women of the village would be going to Evesham to do their shopping.

'How many have we got, Harry?' Dad asked. 'Enough for the rabbit-pie supper?'

'Let's get them on a pole in the dairy first, after I've paunched them,' Mr Bailey replied.

I tipped them out of the bags on to the stone slabs outside the dairy doors. Mr Bailey, with a sharp penknife, paunched them, dropping the paunches into buckets. Dad hocked them, cutting a slit in the hock of the hind leg large enough for the other leg to be pushed through. Then he slid them on to a nut stick the size of a broom handle and he and Mr Bailey lifted the stick of rabbits so that the end of the stick rested on a beam in the low-roofed dairy.

'Just bury the paunches, Fred boy,' Dad said. I carried the buckets to the muck bury near the stable door and, taking a muck fork, dug a hole in the steaming heap of cleanings from the stable and buried the paunches.

We went home to tea smelling of rabbits and gunpowder.

The rabbits were counted and it was decided that if all the folk over sixty-five were going to sit down to a rabbit-pie supper there would be just about enough.

The women of the Chapel met in a sort of committee and decided that it would be best if everyone made pies at home, and brought them steaming hot under tea-cloths in the pie dishes to the Recreation Room where the trestle tables would be lined with the old folk of the village.

The bare planks were covered with table-cloths and the yellow tarnished hard-backed chairs seated the jovial cottage folk. Folk who could all remember the old Queen. They talked of the Boers, the Zulus, the Boxers, Joseph Arch, Gladstone, Lloyd George and the pensions.

At the first meeting of the womenfolk it was pointed out how necessary it was to joint and cook the rabbits before they were put into the pies. As always there were two of the well-meaning folk whose only aim was a successful rabbit-pie supper and who thought they knew better. Of course, they never lived it down.

When the pies were opened the birds didn't begin to sing but the unfortunate seniors of our village didn't really relish half-cooked rabbit, however good the pastry was. Those two rabbit pies were put aside and 'a good time was had by all'.

CHAPTER NINE

Carrants Field

I was nine when Dad took me down the back lane, seated on Tom, the nag, to Carrants Field. We were on our way to horse-hoe the sprouts. In the nag stable where Tom was quartered – a place formerly used for hunters – Dad put the gears, or harness, on the nag.

I noticed that the seventeen-hand cart-horses, heavy legged with feathers covering their great hooves, wore different collars from Tom. Their linings were check patterned like a bookie's jacket; Tom's was navy like Dad's Sunday suit.

For horse-hoeing the usual harness was a set of GO gear. This was a light type of chain harness. Hames back band and light traces with small links. It differed from the ordinary long gears carried by the plough team. No crupper, no hip straps.

Now Dad and Mr Bailey never missed a local farm sale. It was a social occasion. The gathering of the clans of the Vale. They bought ex-WD harnesses which were used to pull the guns by horses in the 1914–18 war. The traces we used on the nag were of wire cable neatly covered with leather. Light yet strong, and the hooks could be strapped in such a way that they never came undone when turning on the headland. Absolutely ideal for horse-hoeing.

I had ridden Tom before and knew a little of the history attached to him. Dad had signed his first cheque when he bought him at the Candlemas Fair.

'It's about time you made a start, Fred. I thought you couldn't go wrong among the sprouts.' Dad carried a short stick in one hand, like a little spreader with binder twine hanging from it which made it look like a small whip.

'What's that for, Dad?' I asked.

'You will see presently.'

The morning hedges were drenched with dew. The sun was up but at a quarter past seven it had not dried the sprouts in Carrants Field. With buckled leggings over my three-quarter-length school stockings I slid off the nag's back. The sprouts were above knee-high to me.

'They will soon dry,' Dad said, 'when the sun gets a bit higher. But meanwhile I don't want to get you wet through.' He then tied some sacking above my leggings to keep my knees dry.

'Now the stick,' he said. 'If I tie this on Tom's mullen (bridle) by the bit, you can guide Tom up between one row and walk up between the next holding the end of the stick, and when I say off a bit, push his head up, you'll understand.'

'What about when you want to keep to the left, Dad?' I asked.

'Oh, then I'll say "To you a bit".'

I'll never forget that first horse-hoeing for me with Dad and the nag in Carrants Field. When the dew had dried off the sprouts by ten o'clock we sat under the hedge and had our lunch. There was really no need for Dad to look at his watch to time us for half an hour. The train to Birmingham passed the level crossing at a quarter to ten and that meant about two more bouts, or twice up the field and twice back and then it would be lunch time. A light engine, as the locals called it, passed at another appropriate time to return to work.

Then the sacking came off my knees and I felt free to walk the long alley of sprouts while Dad held the tails or handles of the horse-hoe.

On the headland as I led Tom into the next row I realised that the stick on the bridle not only made it easier for me to reach and control his bitted mouth but it also enabled me to walk that little distance from those iron-shod hooves of his. Many a boy has gone home with blackened toenails where the keenness of the pulling horse with his iron-shod fore-feet has sunk some little boot into the clay.

It's twenty-five years now since Dad was carried for the last time by four of his former workmen to that little plot by the church tower. God's Acre some call it, and I shall never know now if that first day at horse-hoeing in Carrants Field was meant to be a record-breaking day as acre after acre was hoed. The length of the day! When was the five twenty train going to steam from Beckford station? At every bout, that is, every time we reached the headland near the railroad, Dad lightly spat on his hands as he gripped the horse-hoe tails and quietly said, 'Cup, boy,' Tom walked a steady pace all day. The monotony of rows of sprouts standing in the summer sun like lines of little trees made me turn at each end with a sort of instinct. About twice, apart from meal times, we stopped and swigged Eiffel Tower lemonade from a pint and a half bottle. I saw the young thistles we had cut with the share earlier in the day wilting in the sun as I fetched the bottle, and I picked a few loganberries off a bush in the hedge on the way back. But the five-twenty train eventually came, the little tank engine pulling her three coaches Birmingham way, and Dad undid the traces and left the horse-hoe on the headland.

'Legs ache, Fred boy?' asked Dad. He knew they did and, doubling my left leg, he gave me a leg up on to Tom's back.

'I'll walk across Tun Flun Ten Furlongs. You take the horse around up the lane.'

Tom knew his way up the back lane and one dig in the ribs from my tired feet and he trotted, jolting me. I gripped the hames and what a relief from the endless track of walking the avenues of sprouts in Carrants Field.

Dad was waiting at the stable door and he showed me how to undo the harness, hang up the gear and hold Tom by his forelock as he turned the collar with its sweat-stained lining and after undoing the chinstrap, slipped the mullen over his head. The last thing I noticed Tom lose was the bit from his dusty mouth which had kept him straight all day.

Dad brushed the tide mark of sweat off the nag's shoulders and then we let him loose. Away he galloped up the orchard and rolled over and over on his back under the trees before he trotted through the open gate into Boss Close.

I thought it was lucky for me that Dad broke me into the secrets of leading a horse instead of putting me at the mercy of some clod-throwing carter.

CHAPTER TEN

The Sights and Sounds of Home

It has been said that the composer of the old song, 'Home Sweet Home' never had a home.

Home to a child means most of all Mother. My mother was not homely in the dull sense of the old routine. She adapted herself to the day. Unhurriedly active, best described by the poet Donne, 'So distinctly wrought, that you might almost say her body thought.'

When Mrs Hill had done the morning's housework, trimmed the brass oil lamps, breathed hard on the glass globe and polished it with a duster until it shone, Mother would be ironing on the kitchen table. Heating the irons on the trivet of the oven grate. Then, before tea, she would arrange the patterned mats on the side-board. Mats patterned with pokerwork.

The afternoon light shone on the pink glass ornaments in the whatnot and on the glass droppers. I saw these in every aunt and uncle's house where I went Sunday visiting.

The grandfather clock gave a little warning note at about four minutes to five, then the clock struck and the tea was laid. At half past five Dad arrived and sugared his tea, he'd give it a stir, then ladle a teaspoonful out of his cup, blow on it and taste it. If it needed more sugar he'd measure another half spoonful into it and then drink it.

'Who started this loaf?' He would ask. Perhaps it was me, perhaps my brother Tom. Whoever it was it was always started in the wrong place. 'Never mind,' he'd say, 'just remember another time.' A batch loaf must always be started in the right place, at the bulge. The spoon stood upright in the pot of egg plum jam and the butter made by Mrs Bailey was good and plentiful. I was never up in time in the morning to see Mr Bailey in his shirt-sleeves churning away until the curd came. I saw that later.

In the winter, when the blinds were drawn, our living room soon warmed up with the heat of the fire and the oil lamps. The blinds were khaki-coloured oiled silk material pulled down by a cord and fastened to the window sill. On the end of each cord was a wooden knob shaped like an acorn which could be unscrewed in the middle. Inside the wooden acorn was the knot of the blind string. The egg-shaped bit on the end was to hide the knot. Our blinds were both peep- and draught-proof, but as an extra precaution from the cold where the bow window sills were far apart, a wooden curtain rail was fixed on to the wall. Here the red tasselled curtain was drawn along the wooden-ringed track, completely blotting out the bay window at night.

Before bedtime in winter as Rip stretched his dog's body over the rag rug and Tiddles the tabby cat purred away on the sofa, I sat in the inglenook under the shelf where Dad's twelve-bore cartridges were stacked, one hundred in a box. Boxes with the words 'Crimson Flash' along the side. As the wind howled in the chimney, which was big enough to hold Dad's cob and buggy, the soot fell like black snowballs into the tin where the small brick flue entered the square tower of chimney open to the stars. The ingle was black. Black with tar draught holes which were neck-high to me under the shelf.

A two-hundredweight sack of sprout seed stood dry in the corner. Here Dad scooped and weighed Archer and Bailey's strain and posted it for £1 per pound. Then, like gold, hung another little seed bag labelled Robbin's Blue strain. A sprout variety bought from Evesham by Mr Bailey. This was not for sale. Dad and Mr Bailey talked of it in whispers. Precious seed.

The candles were lit, and after climbing the stairs, my brother and I were soon in bed. The brass knobs on the bedstead shone in the dim light of the candle. It never occurred to me that other boys went to bed in the same way. Seven o'clock. The sound of the church bells were welcome company in a deserted village street. On whist-drive nights I heard the jolly knot of village folk walk past. One man had a wooden leg and it pounded on the road outside.

But the sounds at night when I was nine were few and far between. Sleep came so soon that what noises there were went unheard.

How a feverish cold can make for lonely nights. What a welcome sound was the labouring goods train as it climbed Stanborough incline. I was sorry to hear its chugging become silent as it gained speed and its *diddly dee, diddly da* was lost into the night and Hinton station.

On these rare sleepless nights when the vixen squealed and the dog fox answered, I would wake my brother Tom and ask him to light the candle and tell me the time. Then the owls' hoot was heard. Mr Baldwyn's gleanies called, 'Come back, come back' when a snared rabbit cried in Church Close. A rumble of thunder or the rattle of a late motor bike made the pheasants in the coppice call, 'cock up, cock up.' Nature slept, but slept lightly. What ears the creatures of the wild have.

But how sweet is the sleep of a child. The fantasy of dreams. The security of a tucked-in bed. Only when this is disturbed by a heated brow and fiery throat does he hear the things of the dark village. The whistling plovers' flight explained by my brother Tom. Then the fresh-calved cow bawling in the fields and answered by her calf in the barn. The stamping of horses' steel shoes on the cobbled stable floor down below us where the rats sharpened their teeth on the hard oak beams in the barn and drank from the dripping tap near the milk hut.

But morning came with the daily competition between the long-spurred cocks from their withy perches among the fowls.

People who talk of 'chickens' never saw the light of day among the country folk. Chickens are the little balls of fluff which daintily potter after the victorious broody hen. Hens with straightened neck and ruffled feathers, guard their brood from dogs and little boys, inquisitive little boys, and scratch for worms in the muck bury, and for weed seeds under the thrasher. No, chickens are day olds to a few weeks old. They eat Number One chick food. When the wheat and kibbled maize was broadcast over the patch now bare which once was grass, that was feeding the fowls.

Mother called, 'Biddy, Biddy, Bid, Bid, Bid' and they came from everywhere. When nest boxes had hardly been thought of, in our yard the eggs were collected by me from pot hampers half filled with hay. From the straw mangers of stable and cow shed. From under the manger. A favourite place here for the angry broody to sit on her eggs. Here she sat tight, spread her wings and called 'Cawk, cawk, cawk.'

I was supposed to get her off the eggs or else she would foul the nest. I learnt that quickness was the answer if she didn't respond to Mother's call in the yard, so I picked her up by the tail and tossed her across the stable, then she went, cursing away, towards the rest of the fowls to feed. Sometimes I saw George, Cousin George, who worked an extra team of horses from our stable, riding side saddle with his plough-teams to the fields. Ralph had the main lot of horses at Mr Bailey's yard. George often took two to harrow or drill or plough the land by Great Hill Barn Land where the old men said the stones grew, because though they hauled them off every year for making cart roads, they never seemed to get any less. Everything seemed hurried with Mr Randalls until he had seen his under cowman, George Earles, go stationwards with Min in the milk float with the great seventeen-gallon churns of milk. Then, after breakfast, they fed the calves, cleaned the shed up, while up on the hill Shepherd Tidmarsh had seen his sheep before the village street was aired.

Men got up early. Winter and summer Ralph foddered his horses at about half past five, but the shepherd alone saw the mist from the hill as it lay like a blanket along Carrants Brook. Often, as he climbed Bredon, the stars of the morning twinkled like bits of quick silver – a sort of invoice of morning light.

Of the evening stars, the one I noticed most shone brightly over Cleeve Hill. It came in the twilight, again an indication of the dark to come.

As I walked up the village to Chapel with Dad, or came back from a concert in the Recreation Room, Dad pointed out Jack and his Waggon towards the north, the group of stars known as the Plough. But how vivid, on a keen crisp night when the whole sky was set as a plan of silvern lanterns on a black backcloth, the Plough seemed to me. It's true at certain times of the year the front horse in the team was pitched as if the whole outfit was being driven down a steep slope. But the four corners of the Plough, I am sure, resembled a waggon with the team in front. I saw Ralph coming down Spring Hill those winter nights as I gazed in awe at the wonders of the sky. 'The moon's on his back,' Dad would say. 'It will rain. He carries the water, then tips it out.' A man in the moon. I saw him too. And I saw him with his sheep on the mountains.

And so the sights and sounds of home became so common yet so wonderful. Dad and Mr Randalls getting a hay seed out of a calf's eye. The shepherd marking his ewes after he had mouthed them to determine their age.

'Mark that un on the rump. Her's lost most of her teeth,' he would say to his assistant. 'Her ull have to go.' Then I marvelled at Ralph Pratt as he carried a kerf of hay like a mattress on his head up the ladder into the tallet for the horses' hay rack.

In summer time Mr Bailey out late, shirt-sleeved, driving home the ducks off the moat and from the brook. The green eggs he picked up in the morning before he let them out to feed off the wheat in the duck pond. Eggs all over the place.

Then the Ancona hens, flying like pheasants to Mrs Bailey's call, Mother's call. And the big white eggs they laid.

The activity of the yard was endless as Mr Bailey or Jack Hunting fed the ferrets in the row of cages behind the duck pen. Fed them with a piece of rabbit and bread and milk. The big fitcher ferret Mr Bailey kept, like a pole cat. And everywhere men and boys and horses. Waggons, drays, dogs and guns.

I could not be involved with all this without seeing it to be the be all and end all of everything. Chords have been broken. Life's little day dawned for me in the sheer magic of the farmyard. School? Well, that was a thing which at that time I could not see the end to, but I lived every moment among real men. Men of the village. We shall never see the like of them again.

I no longer wonder why my faith was in things that could be seen. To say that my worship was the worship of the men in the farmyard sums it up.

They were the sights and sounds of Home.

CHAPTER ELEVEN

Goodbye to Bob and Polly

Looking back over my life it's so true that there are turning points standing out like landmarks. In my earliest memories of our road between Beckford and Elmley there were only two or three cars driven at twenty miles per hour. Cars owned by folk from the village; Mr Nicklin, from The Close, had a chauffeur-driven Sunbeam, Mr Church, the dentist, also had a car.

When I had been at Miss Morris's school three or four years, Mr Bailey, Dad's partner, bought a Studebaker twenty-horse-power tourer. George Palmer from Paris, on the hill, soon taught him to drive. This meant that Bob, Mr Bailey's iron-grey pony, was not needed to pull the governess cart to markets and sales. Soon after that Dad made a trip to London with Mr Ernest Roberts of Beckford and bought a Sunbeam sixteen-horse-power tourer. Mr Roberts taught him to drive. Polly, the chestnut mare, grazed Tun Flun – the cow ground – in front of Mr Bailey's house with Bob. I watched with great excitement the change in pattern as Messrs A and B drove to market. Drove to Cheltenham, shopping. They decided to sell their cobs together. I suppose boys were eager to see progress, much the same as today. To me the change from one-horse-power to sixteen- and twenty-horse-power seemed a wonderful thing. But how did my elders feel, I wonder? For together they had bought the governess carts new from Birmingham. And what craftsmanship there was in those Rolls-Royces of the end of the horse age! The shafts were made in a particularly tough wood, shafts which would stand the weight of a heavy cart-horse's clumsy hooves. They sprung like India rubber. Then the wheels with their polished brass hub caps and with every spoke fitted into the felly of the wheel as if it grew there. The rubber tyres were noiseless on the roads.

'Turnouts', these family horse carts were called, and Mr Bailey and Dad had driven Bob and Polly in turnouts to be proud of. Can you think of a more unique combination than that of chestnut and iron grey? Oh no, none of the run-of-the-mill bays and browns for Messrs A and B.

When I saw Ponto polish Polly's brown harness on the wall of our courtyard and make the brass gleam like gold among the leather, no thoughts of regret entered my mind over the Studebaker and Sunbeam takeover. No doubt Ponto polished Bob's harness for Mr Bailey. It was black and shining to blend with the iron grey of Bob.

The day came when the mare and gelding friends of Tun Flun went to what was known as the repository at Cheltenham. Dad sold the complete turnout. Mr Bailey retained the governess cart – perhaps he thought he might need it again one day.

Today I would be sad to see two fast movers of the road disappear in this way. Two fast movers on four legs, that is. Tidy iron-shod hooves which made the sparks fly on the road on many a winter's night.

Min and Tom, the two nags which pulled the market drays and milk float, remained in Tun Flun for me.

In Mr Bailey's motor house under the dovecote stood the coach-built car with its brass lamps – just one more of the kings which were fast taking over our roads.

Cart-horses from our stable were moved to the nag stable where Bob and Polly once stood and one Saturday morning Jack Hunting brought his frail-basket of tools to convert our stable into a motor house – they weren't called garages then – for LX 4415. He widened the doors and made a drive, put up two gate posts and then came an apparent hindrance in his steady work which really had me puzzled. Jack spent a whole day placing a flat stone between the gate posts. 'Why all this fuss over one stone?' I thought. Then, with a brace and an old bit, Jack bored a hole in the stone for the gate fastener to drop into. This focal point had to be measured over and over again until the exact spot was found for the double gates to be fastened securely.

The Sunbeam came over from Grafton where Mr Roberts had housed it and there it stood alongside the stable manger. Grey and black.

How well I remember Dad driving the Sunbeam through the yard and into the motor house the first time, and a trial run up Stanway Hill with Tom and me sheltering in the back seat behind the middle screen of glass under a leather apron. And was it cold at Stow-on-the-Wold!

Wellington boots in the early '20s were rare. I never saw a land-worker wearing them. But when Dad went to London he not only bought the car, he also bought a pair of Wellingtons and what he called a 'hoose-pipe' for cleaning them. Another novelty for me. Hoses on taps I'd never seen before.

Cleaning the car was a ritual. The wooden wheel spokes were brushed and the hose-pipe swilled off most of the dirt and dust. Brasso for the lamps. Brasso for the hub caps. And the hose-pipe proved useful in quite a different way. When the weather was dry the wooden spokes became loose from the hub to the wheel rim. Water from the hose soon tightened them up again and this became a regular treatment in hot, dry weather.

Loose spokes were always referred to as 'talking'. In a waggon, for instance, when the wheels creaked and groaned under the load of hay the carter would say, 'Don't them spokes talk. We shall have to soak the wheels in the horse pond.'

Our car, being grey with black wings complete with klaxon horn, a spare tin of Pratt's petrol locked on to the rubber-covered running board, was never cleaned with any sophisticated polish. Water on the body and Cherry Blossom boot polish on the wings, or mud-guards.

At thirty miles per hour maximum the back axle seemed to sing a tune. 'Warmed up now,' Dad said.

CHAPTER TWELVE

A Chapter of Accidents

A boy who has worked with horses finds no difficulty in understanding what faith is really all about. Horses in general are faithful. I suppose their inbred trust in humans can be taken for granted. I have stood and seen a horse draw a float six miles or more, the driver asleep after a day at the market and pub, the reins hanging loose on the breeching. The traffic passed on the main road. The horse kept on its proper side. Then it would enter the farmyard gate and pull up by the back door of the farm house. It is true the journey had been made many times before, but what price can be put on such devotion and faithfulness. Oh, this is just the fringe of what could be written on how these dumb animals, as my elders called them, co-operated once a confidence was established between them and their masters.

It amazed me as a lad when horses were literally talked through gateways with wide waggon loads and how they knew almost every word spoken in the fields.

'That's about enough for today,' spoken by any ploughman and a six-year-old horse would hold back one step and slacken its traces ready to be unhitched from the plough.

When the Great Welsh Christian Revival was spread like wildfire by Evan Roberts in 1903, it reached the mining valleys. But how do you say that affected the horses? It's said that when the pit pony drivers stopped swearing the ponies refused to work.

These dumb animals have a keen sense of hearing, a detection of mood; akin to how we feel about a house. I, like the majority of boys, sensed an atmosphere in certain houses. Some houses and the people give a welcome that can be felt.

It's a feeling that to sit by the fireside and immediately rest your feet on the coal scuttle would be right. So, as we have felt this, I am sure horses do. If a horse is afraid, or turns away, the fault invariably lies with its master.

To me, among the horses and the men, life was meant to be gay and free from blight. To me the words of the old Lambeth adage rings just as clear through the hedgerows:

> What a merry man?
> Let him do all he can
> To entertain his guests
> With wine and pleasant jests,
> Yet if his wife do frown
> All merriment goes down.

Dad was a merry man. Not that he often laughed, but that twinkle in his eye had a power that gave life capital letters. I always fancied him more at home assessing a bunch of cattle than with horses.

One mare we had named Bonnie, deep chocolate in colour, was described by Ralph the carter in his inimitable way: 'Her's the sort of oss you can put dependence in.' One blistering hot afternoon in July when I was about eight, I went with Dad and Bonnie to fetch an empty waggon from the Little Dewrest. The country roads maintained by the Rural District Council were dusty, as they always were in summer. Tarmac had not reached our village. I'd seen the sharp-edged Clee Hill stone rolled in by the steam roller. Then the smaller stones rolled in on top. These stones were softer and crunched under the roller's weight followed by the horse-drawn water cart. The surface was as MacAdam had introduced years ago, a mixture of gravel, soil, sand, small stones, which cemented together with water and the roller's weight. Dusty in summer, muddy in winter. It was down the Groaten, the way to the station, Dad led Bonnie harnessed with Fillers Gears.

Before we started from the stable, Dad hoisted me up into the cart saddle and told me to hold the hames which stuck up like two brass-knobbed handles above Bonnie's collar. Clarice, my younger sister, sat behind. It was uncomfortable sitting astride the cart saddle but the prospect of the afternoon was pleasant. Dad, shirt-sleeved and wearing his Panama hat, led Bonnie past Mr Nicklin's late pea pickers who were at work over the railway bridge. I knew that when we arrived at the little meadow all three of us would ride back in the waggon. The main Cheltenham road had just been tarred and gritted. County Council job. The tar shone black through the patches of road where the grit was sparse. Bonnie's hooves left marks like half-moons in the sun-drenched surface. Dad walked alongside and Bonnie met the few cars and occasional steam waggons quite unconcerned.

Two hundred yards to go, just opposite the Middle Dewrest gateway, the cart saddle slipped round, the girth straps being slack and I fell headlong, hitting my head on the road. Clarice fell on the grass. The cut temple above my left eye oozed blood and the wound was full of the new-laid grit off the road.

As if it was meant to be, Mr Bailey arrived on his bike and he sat me under the hedge and mopped the blood with his handkerchief. 'Borrow your bike, Harry,' Dad said and went off home on it for the car. Bonnie stood still in the road for a while and then turned in at the next gateway and stood by the waggon. Just as if she knew. When Dad arrived in the car, Mr Bailey looked after Bonnie and the waggon while we went to Evesham to the doctor.

Cuts in the '20s called for iodine and the doctor's iodine was thick like mustard. The doctor probed the grit from the wound and washed it clean and the usual iodine, pink lint wadding and cotton wool and bandages were all fixed with a safety pin. I looked like a wounded soldier. The doctor had put a couple of stitches in and Dad said, 'We are going to London in a few days, will that be all right?'

'Take him to a doctor there, Mr Archer, and have the stitches out.'

Coming down the steps from the surgery, we met Mr Anderson of Watkins and Simson, the firm most of our pea seed came from. 'Hello, Tom,' he said to Dad, 'what's young Fred been up to?'

Dad said, 'Oh, he's just fallen off a horse.'

'Fallen from a horse,' Mr Anderson said. 'I never thought that Fred Archer would fall from a horse.' We got back to the car and I asked Dad why I shouldn't fall from a horse. Dad laughed and explained that Fred Archer was once a famous jockey; in fact the most famous of jockeys.

As Dad had promised, our family went to London a few days afterwards. What a reach to the beyond it seemed to me! Soon the car was humming away along the five-mile drive past Broadway Tower. Broadway Tower had up until that morning been my boundary. Past that was foreign ground unexplored.

Being late July, Dad had loaded the luggage carrier at the back of the car with a withy pot hamper to hold the green peas, strawberries, etc., we were taking to my cousin, Nellie Breeze. Well, her name was Wickens now since she was married with a family. Jim Breeze, her father, Dad never stopped talking about. He had been a guard on the London and North Eastern Railway and was killed by an express train. I never saw him, but apparently he was the sort of man everyone liked.

Nellie Wickens' husband was a fodder merchant in Tooting. He cut the chaff, ground the corn for the horses on the London streets. Nellie kept a milliner's shop. She trimmed hats in those days when one hat could be trimmed so many times according to fashion. I remember the fruit and flowers on those hats, harvest festival-like hats.

I was proud of our car and, sitting in the back of this open tourer, my brother, sister and I were sheltered by a second windscreen with an apron around our legs. This screen had two side panels of glass which could be adjusted by thumb screws. I watched the speedometer which was numbered up to sixty m.p.h., but at twenty m.p.h. a red line was drawn. Dad kept the needle on twenty-five m.p.h. pretty constant. It was tea-time at Tooting when Dad manoeuvred our horseless coach with shining brass radiator and headlamps into one of cousin George Wickens' disused stables.

George had been filling sacks of mixed horse fodder all day. His oil engine was turning the pulleys and belts of the machines. Nellie was proud of her Uncle Tom (Dad) with his car. A Sunbeam from Wolverhampton. 'Nice, Uncle,' she said, 'I'm longing for a ride in it.' Nellie was stout like all the Archers I had met. Her mother, Alice, was Dad's sister.

Sunday, the day following, we were taken to some Citadel of the Salvation Army. Here was an opportunity to listen to one of the top-class bands. I'd seen before the Army Crest of Blood and Fire and the photograph of the old General Booth whose bearded face and piercing eyes seemed to say something louder than words.

I remember Mother was a bit shocked because Nellie opened her shop for a while on Sunday morning. The next day was August Bank Holiday and her shop would be closed all day.

'I thought about a run down to Brighton today,' Dad said.

'That would be fine, Uncle,' Nellie said. 'I've only been by charabanc.'

Quite early we started. Dad never kept what he called 'quality hours'. Mother and Dad sat in the front and Nellie and her two children, and we three children, sat in the back. Even in 1924 that road was busy on a Bank Holiday. Charabancs were in the majority. Those long coaches, high off the road, had rows of seats crossways, everybody facing forwards. At the end of each row, in fact at both ends, was a door. The passengers were, like us, open to the sky, except when it rained when the hood of canvas and hickory wood was pulled over the top from the back. Painted at the back were names like Pleasure Boat, the Brighton Queen, etc.

The trippers waved their sandwiches and bottles of beer as we passed them. August Bank Holiday had to be observed, made the most of in those days. No doubt some of the folk remembered that August Monday ten years before when war was declared.

We parked by the pier at Brighton and sat with the

straw-hatted crowd on the sands and ate our sandwiches. The parasols went up over the ladies. Dad walked in sandshoes and came back from the pier loaded with bottles of pop. We paddled and dug between the bathing machines. They looked like our shepherd's hut to me, but Mother said they were for people to change into their bathing costumes. Not even a bare chest was exposed to the sun by the men. The ladies' costumes had little frilly skirts and were as black as crows. The sun poured down on the one day's worship of the English Channel.

So this was Brighton with the chatter of us all near the pier as children swarmed like bees around Punch and Judy and men, some crippled by the war, squatted on the hot asphalt of the promenade with their paintings. Street artists, Dad said they were as he tossed a copper into their caps under the sea wall. Then there was the smell of the donkeys. The shouting of the ice-cream men.

We sat the afternoon away, watched the steamers tie up at the pier. Dad decided to fetch some ice-cream. 'They make it with custard powder now you know, Lil,' he said to Mother. 'I want some of the real stuff, real ice-cream.' I followed him past one stall and then another, but found after a while I was following someone else's Dad. So lost a boatman looked after me, dried my tears, and then Dad came, thanked the boatman and turned to me saying, 'You had us worried to death, you young mortal.'

Nellie said that it would take two hours to return to Tooting and we ought to be in bed soon after eight.

At six that evening we all took our places in the car and headed for London. Since there was not enough room on the back seat, I sat among the feet of the passengers up against the central windscreen. It was a lovely evening, but unfortunate that all the trippers decided to start back at six o'clock. Dad steered past one chara after another. The car's engine, all sixteen-horse-power, purred as it took the straight roads over the Downs. Near Reigate, we started to pass yet another chara, but, without a signal, it pulled out as it passed some cyclists.

Running out of road, Dad took to the grass verge where unfortunately heaps of stones had been dropped at intervals for road-making.

We mounted the first and with 'Hey up' from me went over the top of it, then over the top of the second, finishing up perched on top of the third one. A huge joke, we children thought, now we shall be late getting home.

At that moment, as if he knew what was going to happen, an AA man appeared. 'Do you belong to the AA, sir?' he said. Dad said, 'No.' The patrol man got out his book, explaining it would be a good thing to join. Dad signed the cheque and the man put a sticker on the windscreen. Then, lying on his back under the front of the car, he said, 'I'm afraid you have a broken spring, sir. I'll arrange to get you home and have the car towed to a garage.'

So we sat waiting for a taxi. It seemed hours, but eventually it came. Home-bound cars whizzed by. Then just as we were about to get in the taxi some chap driving a two-seater car with a dickie seat, gawped at our car on the heap of stones and drove bang into the back of the taxi. The passenger, a lady in the dickie seat, catapulted out into the road and broke her leg. The taxi then took her to hospital and we waited for another one.

It was twelve o'clock when we arrived at Tooting. Cousin George made some tea and, before we went to bed, Mother told me when I said my prayers to thank God we were not all killed.

The garage where the AA took our car to was quite near Tooting. Next morning I remember going by bus with Dad and my brother Tom to see the car. The man at the garage said that the repairs would take two or three days. The leaves in the spring were broken and I fancy he had to get the parts from Wolverhampton. Dad had already claimed on his insurance, but found that the company had just gone bankrupt. There was nothing to do but to pay.

Motor accidents were news. Ours, however minor, was reported in a London evening paper.

'Tom Archer, an Evesham farmer, drives his car along the grass verge over two heaps of stones.'

Our next visit to the garage was to fetch the car away mended fit for the road. Dad drove proudly through London. I suppose we had gone about half a mile before a mounted policeman, with a shiny spike on his helmet and waxed moustache, held up a white-gloved hand.

'What the nation is the matter now?' Dad said, as he pulled up near the kerb.

'Where's your number plate, governor?' the mountie said.

Dad got out, looked at the gap between the springs and no number plate was there.

'Well I'm blowed, the garage man has not put it back on,' he told the PC.

'You'll have to do something about it. It's an offence you know, I could summons you.'

The policeman added, 'Up from the country, ay? A farmer, I suppose.'

Dad looked a bit crestfallen and replied. 'A broken down one you could call me.' Mind, that's not how he felt but Dad could put on an act. So many times he has told me when you are on a spot, never ride the high horse; it pays to eat humble pie.

'You'll have to get a temporary plate before you drive any farther.'

'I'll do that,' Dad said and he went into a greengrocer's shop and got a piece of cardboard and, over the counter, he and the greengrocer wrote in bold capitals a number plate – LX 4415. Once it was fixed with string (we always carried string) we were under way once more.

About another half-mile Tooting way, two policemen flagged us down from the pavement.

'Now what next?' Dad said as he got out of the car. A Cockney voice said, 'Can't you read the speed-limit signs? You've passed two; there's a twelve m.p.h. limit along this road.'

'Oh, I'm sorry,' Dad said. We must have been belting along at twenty m.p.h.

'From the country, I suppose,' the PC said, and I wondered however they knew. I suppose it does show. Was it Dad's Panama hat or his Gloucestershire accent? Maybe it was the rosy cheeks from years in the open air. We drove off very slowly, and I fancy kept the speedometer needle around twelve m.p.h. the rest of the way to Tooting.

The next August Monday, the Brighton road was left to the charabancs and Dad never ventured along the track again. As for cousin Nellie, I did say the Archers were all stout. Not being told about these things, I had no idea she was what is known as 'expecting'. She had another daughter, Kath, soon after Brighton.

The next day a London doctor took the stitches out of the horseshoe-shaped cut on my left temple. Believe it or not, his name was Doctor Cob.

CHAPTER THIRTEEN

The Wireless

'What are the wild waves saying?' was the slogan at the very beginning of music on tap. I thought of wireless waves as the tide at last coming in, coming into our village seventy miles from the sea with white horses hitting the rocks.

In a way the tide did come in that day when Percy Wigley made his first wireless set and Ray Priday with cat's whisker and crystal linked us with London for the very first time.

Stirring times, you may say. I well remember going with my brother to Ray Priday's cottage and together holding the headphones and hearing Big Ben strike six o'clock.

'It's nothing but works of the Devil,' said one man the other side of Bredon Hill.

'No doubt it ull upset the weather,' was Uncle George's prediction. That was what he used to say about changing the clocks. He used to talk of 'God's time'.

Country folk who had sung around the piano and held concerts in the Reading Room were suspicious of the wireless.

Ernest Roberts, a dab hand at anything mechanical, started making three-valve sets for the folk who could afford twenty pounds. It took all day to install one. The high aerial, the insulators and the sunken bucket for the earth wire were all a part of the early wireless outfits. A low-tension battery, weighing fifty-six pounds and a high-tension one, then the coils which were changed for different stations. 2 LO seemed to be our station when our set arrived.

I can still see the horn loudspeaker on the dresser, the set on a small table and the big battery on the floor.

Dad turned the knob which moved the coils closer together

or farther apart. Squeals came from the horn speaker, then oscillations up and down the scale. A bit of practice, then Peter Eckersley's voice was loud and clear. 'This is 2 LO calling, 2 LO . . .' on so many metres. Then we sat around and listened to John Henry and Blossom, a comedy act. We were in touch with London and Birmingham. Shepherd Tidmarsh and his wife came with Uncle George some evenings.

'Well I'm dalled,' the shepherd said as he looked out at the starry night. 'A hundred miles to London and I've heard Big Ben.'

Mr Bailey bought a five-valve set and when he wanted to listen alone he wore the headphones. Listening to a play one evening, he told me, he nodded off to sleep to be rudely awakened by the piercing notes of a soprano screaming in his ears.

The shepherd looked at the sky at night and still wondered, as we all did, how this marvel had been born. The news, saxophones, whether one liked it or not, jazzed throughout the village.

In the little community of three hundred people I often thought as we sang to the Chapel harmonium Wesley's hymn, 'Oh for a thousand tongues to sing', what an odd wish that was. Before the wireless there was music of a kind in our village. Children's voices, singing happily to Mrs Church's piano, could be heard from the school; songs were sung at a village concert by ploughmen and shepherds. Shakespeare said, 'A man that has no music in himself nor is moved with concord of sweet sounds is fit for treasons, strategems and spoils.' There are, of course, exceptions to his theory. Dr Johnson, for instance, was once told that a certain piece of music was difficult and he replied that he 'regretted that it was not impossible'.

So at prep. school when I had the chance to learn to play the piano I refused. My brother took up the challenge and stayed late on Friday nights, having his tea at Liley's in the High Street and coming home on the seven o'clock train. Clarice, my sister, learnt on Miss Kimpton's piano at a house in the village known as Hulses. Cissy, I thought it was, for a boy to learn 'Afton Water' and things I considered sentimental. But here I lived in partial isolation, longing to press my lips to a cornet or trombone and play something which stirred – by Sousa or Elgar. Every boy's ambition to be a man was present within me. But no, the tinkle of the piano had no appeal. I was intensely fond of all kinds of music, with the exception of the piano, which I thought to be a very feminine instrument. When John Eliss sang from his endless repertoire under the corrugated iron roof of the old army hut, Miss Baldwyn played the piano.

I found music in the things around me. In nature as the birds sang undisturbed by the jingle of horse harness. The wind wailing down our chimney. The cawing of rooks. The leaves whispering on the trees. The blacksmith singing 'Drink to me only with thine eyes' as he nailed the shoes on to Bonnie or Captain. All these things were music to me, real music. As real as stewed rabbit on a Wednesday or fried mackerel on a Friday.

I discovered that every trade and occupation had its own special music. The boatman when he went on trips to the seaside. The miner, emerging from the bowels of the earth. The shepherd, tending his sheep on the hills, and the ploughman with his team of horses, turning the rich dark soil. Song has been the companion of labour since the world began, 'the mother of sympathy' and 'the handmaid of religion'. The bride goes to her marriage, the labourer to his work, the old man to his last long rest, each accompanied by appropriate immemorial music.

As David soothed Saul with his music when Saul was in one of his moods, so on these frosty mornings when the voice travelled clearly for half a mile, I heard Ralph singing in the furrow behind the plough-team, 'We are all jolly fellas who follow the plough'. That was good. It was not quite right to say that 'God's in his Heaven and all's right with the world', but I knew that Ralph's ploughing was going smoothly and that he had tobacco in the tin box in his corded waistcoat pocket.

Here, as the birds followed the newly turned earth and the larks were singing above, music did have charm.

About that time Paul Robeson came with his negro spirituals, his labour songs. 'Old Man River' conjured up in my mind how unjust labour could be. Of course, the wireless had changed everything.

I still went some Sunday nights to listen and join in when I could to the singing around Aunty Lucy's cottage organ. Cousin Mary played and pedalled away at the carpeted pedals. How did she know which stops to pull out? Black and shining with white fronts, the stops looked like a secret witchcraft to me.

The number of cottagers who owned a melodeon surprised me. As the harp was to the Welsh, so the melodeon cheered many a home in our English village; and who cared what mistakes were made? It was music. Music of our village. Not the magic of the cottage organ or harmonium, but here was a need fulfilled. A contribution to life. The simple life. I think we were pitied then. But we did not need pity.

Becoming more used to music was inevitable when Dad chose the evening programme on the wireless. Like me, he liked the sound of brass. We listened to the colliery bands playing their rousing marches. From the horn of our loud-speaker I heard the birds sing as Albert Ketelby's 'In a Monastery Garden' was played. How that alone gave me a different idea of a monastery is hard to say. It changed everything from a walled-in mystery to a place of peace. As did Gracie Fields change a city slum with her 'Sally in our Alley'. But the most wonderful thing of all was 'The way of a man with a maid'.

Dad liked 'Just a song at twilight, when the lights are low'. For me, Elgar's 'Pomp and Circumstance No. 4' put me on a higher plane. I wondered if it was because Elgar breathed the Worcestershire air that he had this feeling for us who lived within sight of the Malverns.

One Sunday, as I sat on a green-covered chair with my elbows on the oval veneered mahogany table, Gipsy Smith made a broadcast. When he sang 'Tell me the old, old story of Jesus and His love' the tears trickled down my cheeks and I was ashamed. Ashamed because I knew of his humble birth in Epping Forest; and touched by his voice which thrust a message straight to me.

CHAPTER FOURTEEN

Corner-stones

Along with other boys of the village, I mingled, grey-jerseyed with the corduroyed shepherds, cowmen and carters. There were always these staid men around, standing, leaning, often bent, but corner-stones. Men who gave a sense of eternity to an unexplained world.

This was the very breath of country life where men like Ralph Pratt worked long hours with his four-horse team turning the clay clats or clods with the scuffle. Here was a man slight in build but strong in heart; a philosopher who sized up crops, wind and weather.

His horses formed a team. Ralph was one of a team of stalwarts of the '20s.

As I heard Shepherd Tidmarsh's bronchial cough when he crossed the rickyard, bent under a sack of sheep cake or with four hurdles on his back, I knew that he worked according to the weather and the season. No need to tell him how to spend a wet day on the land. He would be found in the granary, stripped to his shirt sleeves, turning the wheel on the cake grinder. The kibbled linseed and cotton-seed oil cake flowed in a constant stream into the bushel measure as one slab after another was fed into the kibbler. No, bronchitis never stopped the shepherd. He worked, he joked and the scent of his twist tobacco smoke as it swirled in blue eddies around the beams was just one of the little pleasures of his life.

As the years at prep. school passed and Fred Randall's health failed, Tom Whittle became cowman for Mr Bailey and Dad. I became particularly attached to him because he worked a lot of his time around the buildings of Stanley Farm. Here he foddered the winter yarded cattle. Suckled the calves, three on each cow, in the long shed.

I well remember sitting on the manger edge with him while the white-faced dark red calves sucked and bunted the patient Shorthorn cows.

Tom carried a little nut stick and when a cow kicked at a newly born calf of a week or so old he would say, 'Now then, old girl, stand still, ull ya?' The cow would rattle the chain, turn and show the whites of her eyes, half expecting a stroke from Tom's stick.

''Tis all done by kindness,' he said to me, 'and if we can't manage her we ull send for that man from London.'

'Who is that man from London?' I often thought.

Then the weaned calves, who had bawled themselves hoarse calling for the milk they no longer needed, pulled at the best hay from the hay rack and ate their cake from the troughs. I was glad they were hoarse after so many noisy nights when calves bawled and cows mooed.

Tom split withy sticks on wet days and made rick pegs for thatching the hayricks. I suppose the day men worked long hours too, but they did get their weekends off.

Cousin George, always up with the lark, whistled down a deserted village street at four o'clock on summer mornings. He stopped his bike outside our garden by the yew tree and called, 'Uncle Tom.' Dad got up ready to take a car load of strawberries and peas to the early morning market at Cheltenham in the back of the Sunbeam.

In our village, where the water supply came from roadside standpipes, George was first out on a frosty morning in the winter with a kettle of hot water to thaw out the taps. Others followed with their buckets. I think they waited for him to thaw those taps out. A great man for the morning was George, and, of course, Mr Bailey was always about at first light or before. Out with Ralph in the stable, giving the orders for the day.

What a pattern this makes for me now. There was a place for everyone and everybody in their place.

Some say they can be independent of everything, but men who were my corner-stones gave life a purpose. Was the purpose of life only what religion offered? I think not. The humble job well done was a lesson to me that could not be learned at school or Chapel. These men to me were the backbone of life among the stock and crops of 500 acres farmed and market-gardened by Mr Bailey and Dad. The men who appeared to make things tick in Ashton were the farmers and landowners themselves – and a few of the gentry.

To me they fell into two categories. First, Mr Nicklin who owned and farmed with his younger son a fair slice of this land I tread. An iron-master from the Black Country who fell in love with Paris, a hamlet on the hill, as a weekend retreat, years before I was born. Then he bought a lovely black and white house known as The Close. He employed two gardeners, won prizes with roses and daffodils, and when I knew him he travelled first-class to Birmingham after Mr Ellis, his chauffeur, had driven him to the station. He bought land and his son, Charlie, farmed it. There was something rather frightening about him to us boys as he boarded our school train, immaculately dressed with a king-size cigar. Known as 'The Old Gentleman' he was respected more than anyone in the village.

In his class was Dr Roberson, MRCS, who took a big part in Church and State. Then John Baldwyn was the last of a line of aristocrats who had farmed here for six hundred years. These, plus Mr Hughes, the artist, comprised the top-brass of Ashton Village. These men played their different roles well, preventing the parish from falling into a state of mediocrity. But it really could not have done that completely, because there were many who, although of slightly lesser standing, nevertheless would have been able to conduct the parish pump politics of that day.

Charlie Nicklin everyone loved. His wit was not appreciated by me until much later. Bernard, his brother, had been a genius in steel but chose to gamble with the market-garden crop down the Groaten. I suppose JB, as he was known, in preference to Bernard, could have accomplished anything when he put his whole heart into it. A student of prophecy, preacher, staunch churchman, inventor, thinker. Truly a great man.

These years, less than ten since the end of the Great War, were years when the yeoman farmer still had a part to play in village and farming life. I think naturally of the folk I liked. The fact is, there was no one I disliked.

Mr Hugh Clements was an excellent example of a yeoman farmer. He milked cows and employed one man. His wife kept the Post Office and Stores and they also had a Bake House. I often stood with Frank and watched Mr Clements bring the hot fresh batch-cakes out on the peel, steaming and wholesome. His family delivered the milk and his forty ewes and the ram grazed around the beeches of the Cuckoo Pen while his store cattle lay on Holcombe Nap. When, today, people talk of specialisation well, Mr Clements' eggs were graded into several baskets and Mrs Clements made superb butter. And so back in about 1925 Mr Hugh Clements, with his dray, laden with sheep rails or racks, pulled by a bit of good horseflesh, was a familiar sight down our village street on market days. Sometimes he would be loaded with a bunch of fat lambs or store lambs. On another day a calf would be lying on the strawed bed of the dray as he stood at the front holding the leather reins on his way to Evesham, Beckford or Tewkesbury. A genial man was Mr Clements, like Dad and Mr Bailey. Quick on the trigger at the running rabbit. A keen follower of football and cricket and, most important to me, he liked boys. He seemed to understand us.

He often told me of the club feasts in his father's yard. The outdoor quoits in the garden of the pub. He had probably forgotten more about the making of good cider than most people ever knew. Then he grew osiers down in the withy bed for making hampers. There was in Ashton at that time a number of men who bought and sold orchards of fruit – mainly apples – Mr Clements was one of them and so was Mr Bell from the Plough and Harrow. He was a man who rode a motor-bike and climbed ladders despite having only one leg.

John Baldwyn's sons, Jack, Tom and Will followed various occupations. Jack was a market gardener at Paris. He grew cherries and daffodils. Tom farmed the Croft, a little holding of fruit where he kept a few cows and pigs and made hay with Bill Allen in the Languet, a hill field. He was a pig killer and was a most interesting character.

'I pick the fruit when it's mella,' he told me (in other words 'ripe').

Tom was a jovial type. A bachelor who made some of the most potent cider the village has ever tasted. I didn't see him often as he and his brother Will lived in a backwater under the hill.

Will had a game leg, but what an authority he was on local history. He collected rates and did people's income tax accounts, that is to say, those few people who paid tax. He cycled round with a walking stick strapped on the cross-bar so that when he had to walk he could do so without too much trouble. Chairman of the Parish Council and knowing every footpath and bridleway in the village, Will was a mine of information as he slowly deliberated his opinion, which was so often right. Hours I've spent with Will and Tom, and learnt once more that the life, the background, the breeding if you like, came out so naturally in their talk.

Interesting men, Jack, Tom and Will were some of the last of the true yeomen who fed their pigs, bred game-cocks for roasting, and their sister Kate churned the butter and scrubbed the white kitchen table. And here we have the men and women who cherished their independence but who helped the less fortunate.

At the end of Cotton's Lane, a lane named after the second oldest family in the village, stands a large stone house known as The Manor. I learnt, as I listened to the old farm hands, how years ago Mr James Cotton found a medal in the garden of The Manor. Legend has it that Admiral Vernon once lived there, he who won the sea battle at Porto Bello. 'Old Grog' he was called because it was he who introduced rum for the sailors to drink to prevent scurvy. It's odd that another Mr Vernon lived there and farmed that land after the First World War. Then Mr and Mrs Frank Field came.

Frank was lean and active, with a whimsical smile. His father had been one of the more prosperous market gardeners of Evesham.

Mr and Mrs Field had their car at about the same time as us. They both drove. It was most unusual to see a lady driving a car in 1925. I saw the produce of Mr Field's farm pass our house on the way to the station. Alec Barnett was carter and he came down the hill with a great yellow farm cart stacked high with sprouts or peas according to the season. The thing that struck me about Frank Field was the fact that he never took half measures over anything. His maxim was that if you plant a couple of acres of peas and the price is high, you don't make a fortune. Of course, if the trade was bad, the loss was small. Frank would plant in a big way and when the returns were high he clicked. I'd say Frank was a man willing to have a go.

He worked hard and I saw him in his prime on the headland of a pea field talking to Dad. I can still see that mischievous twitch of his nose and the innocent little snigger he uttered as the carter with the pea drill drew the furrows up and down and developed a kink in the rows.

'More peas in a crooked row, Tom,' he'd say to Dad.

Then the ground set hard after the Cambridge roll had levelled the land and the peas couldn't push through the soil. Tom Whittle worked for him before he came to us and advised Mr Field to run a set of heavy harrows over the planted land. The next day on his way to work, Tom told us how 'Master Field's peas are up in rows this morning.'

Did anyone ever grow such sprouts as Frank Field did in the Big Ground? I doubt it. Sprouts like coconuts – Byrd Bros. strain – grew one year when cousin Tom picked the equivalent of fourteen nets in thirty-five minutes. In those days they were put in hampers so it was actually seven hampers in thirty-five minutes.

Mrs Maud Field, a member of a Worcestershire family going back to the Commonwealth, was a particularly good-looking lady. She dressed well and was a good Samaritan to many of the villagers. She and Bunch Baldwyn used to take blancmanges and beef-tea to the sick of the parish. Reliable, unassuming, not patronising in any way. It's not the value of these little gifts in sickness which matters most, but the thought that someone cares.

I have often said that everything stopped in our village when an important football match was being played in the Wynch. Frank Field would be a little late with his milking; Dad and Mr Bailey sacrificed the afternoon with their guns after fur and feather.

It seemed to me on those idyllic Saturdays that life as it was known, the life of sweat and toil, suddenly stopped as young and old climbed the Wynch stile and put twopence into Hugh Clements' collecting box – the price of admission to a cup tie. One thousand people around a village pitch was a sight to remember.

It is worth recording that in those post-war years when physiotherapy was never talked of, the Ashton trainer rubbed pulled muscles with embrocation made in pint and a half bottles from linseed oil, turpentine and beaten eggs. As I stood on the line and watched and noticed the use come back into strained limbs and smelt the yellow balm, it seemed that once again the corner-stones of Ashton were at work as play resumed. A dislocated knee was put back into place in a brace of snaps by Mr Jim Cotton, a man of so many parts.

The rare broken leg, and everyone's eyes saddened when the player took a journey through the gate by Percy Attwood's stable, lying on overcoats on one of Charlie Moor's hurdles, to Harry Stratford's carrier lorry which took the unlucky player to hospital.

One often talks of getting rid of class distinction. In 1925 at village football everyone seemed to be on one level. They shouted for victory and the side rarely let them down. Folklore like The Simple Life are common topics today. Forty-seven years ago when father told son and grandfather told father, life's meaning seemed different. Life was not so cheap. When everyone said that Arthur Thomson from the Wood Farm once bowled out W.G. Grace, that was no more than the sort of thing expected from an Ashton man.

So I saw our parish as a compact unit as close as a hen to her chickens, with the mature birds strutting around guarding the patch as a cock robin claims its own garden.

CHAPTER FIFTEEN

Highways and By-ways in 1926

It was a crisp frosty morning on the first day of January when I first rode my bike into Evesham. The sort of day when the roadside hedges hung heavy with rime, or hoar frost. The main road glistened as the weak rays of the sun reflected rainbow colours from the stones. A scarf-and-gloves morning. I went with my brother, Tom, and John Cave to get a sixpenny haircut at Greens, ready for school the next week.

At Gipsies' Corner a tramp was drumming up some tea in a blackened cocoa can over a wood fire.

'Happy New Year,' I shouted for about the sixth time that morning.

He swore and blasphemed at me as I rode slowly by on my eighteen-inch frame Crown bicycle. I wondered why as he cursed the Government as he stood over the fire, his war ribbons pinned to his shabby overcoat.

'Isn't it a happy New Year?' I thought. Then John told me I shouldn't have wished it to a tramp. But aren't there always tramps? Don't they choose to live that way and won't they always be with us, like the gipsies? Gipsies' Corner is one of their camping grounds. Among the withies I had often seen their hooped or tilted waggons and the ponies grazing the roadside verges.

I learnt a lesson that day. A lesson that gipsies chose their way of life in the open air. But tramps were so often on the road because of unemployment and the after-effects of the war. I spoke to them often in Thurness Shed where they slept, cooked a few potatoes from some farmer's potato bury. Drank their tea with condensed milk. Ate their potatoes with bully beef. These men were clean on the whole. They shaved with open razors, looking at their faces with a broken piece of looking-glass, glass coloured red at the back. I was fascinated when they smoked tea leaves instead of tobacco. 'Never do this boy,' one man of the road told me. 'Bad for the heart see,' and as he said it, he held his heart. His breathing was bad too. He coughed and wheezed and muttered, 'Mustard Gas.'

It was only then that Hardy's words came to me. Miss Morris had given to me a love of poetry of a rural nature. Thomas Hardy and Barnes were favourites of mine. Hardy wrote so truly in 1917 of the evolution of man for better or worse. The words seemed apt as I talked to the Men of the Road, men who had stood between us and the invader for four years. Now what was Hardy really thinking as he penned:

> After 2000 years of Mass
> We've got as far as poison gas.

That New Year's Day had followed a spell of frost and snow. The thaw had swelled the River Avon as the water drained from the ditches and brooks of Warwickshire and Worcestershire.

The Workman Gardens flooded and, as we rode along the Waterside, the brown earth-stained river lapped against the whale's jaw-bone which forms an archway under the trees. Mother had told me so often of the Evesham man who harpooned the descendant of Jonah's three-day hide-out. We stopped and stared as the road began to flood. We debated the Jonah story but decided that this mammal could have swallowed a Jersey cow.

I liked the Waterside that day and watched the boatmen ready to ferry the people on foot towards Hampton.

The iron-tyred market gardeners' drays rattled through the rising water. We rode our bikes along the pavement. We hurried home. It seemed to me that the main roads were already catering for the cars. Smooth and tarred and even.

Only Sedgeberrow Bank and Bridge Street were purposely kept rough to enable the dray horses to grip with their shoes as they drew the loaded vehicles up the hills.

Even the station road to Ashton, or the Groaten as it was known, was tarred and smooth to slide on when icy. The Company, or the railway, gritted the bridge for the horse traffic. Draymen carried shovels in such weather and scattered the grit from roadside heaps.

The caravan of drays to the two markets loaded with garden produce was a sight. The noise of iron-shod wheels in that pre-pneumatic age sounded like a goods train, where the guard's van never came in sight.

The cobble-stones still remained outside Hamilton and Bells, and at the near-by King's Head the drays jolted over the cobbles when the draymen shut out their horses, nags, ponies, stabled them, leaving their empty drays on that wide area outside.

One gentleman was ill in a fine house in the High Street. I believe he had pneumonia. I saw sawdust from the timber yard spread inches deep on the patch of road outside the house. The powdered wood silenced the dray wheels as they passed. He recovered and the Council roadmen swept the sawdust away. But up that same street we stood hatless that last year at prep. school, as Evesham's prominent photographer, for whom I had sat sailor-suited with the family in his studio to be photographed, made his last journey along the street. Why does this stick in my memory! It was no ordinary funeral. He was to be cremated. A rare thing in 1926. I conjured up in my young mind how it would be done. It was the talk of the town and we didn't understand.

But all roads were not like the main roads. The narrow road to Kersoe, which was our usual Sunday afternoon walk, was muddy in winter, dusty in summer, and still had a patch of green grass up the middle where the dray and car wheels didn't run.

It was a delight to me to lean on the rails of the little Brook Bridge just past Ayles Acre Bank and put one foot into Worcestershire and one in Gloucestershire.

My mother, Lily Archer

Fred, aged fifteen

Uncle George on a Chapel outing to Weston-super-Mare

Tom, Clarice and Fred

Clarice, Dad and Fred, aged twenty-three

Stanley Farm

Shepherd Tidmarsh with his sheep

Aunt Lucy with Mrs Cotton, her grandson Denis Hunting, and
Gertie Stanton

Not only was this the county boundary, but the district council boundary and the parish boundary. Here the roadmen met. Here the road surface changed. Worcestershire was over the border and some sort of blue stone was on the surface of the road. It was possibly Clee Hill. Here the policemen met and compared notes. I felt daring as I crossed into another county; it was a sort of exploration into another world.

Back in our village street, Stodge, our roadman, kept the grass cut and the edges of the road trimmed, unstopped the gouts, or stone drains, filled the potholes and swept.

On windy March days the dust from his broom lay on the brown leaves of last year's blackberry, like volcanic particles windswept from an exploding crater.

From the Romans to MacAdam, very little had been done to improve our roads. Ashton village street and the road to Beckford was metalled in the MacAdam style. No barrels of tar or lumps of pitch were used to bind the surface here.

I watched with interest when the whole stretch of road from Cottons Lane to the Grafton Boundary was remade. Mr William Spires and his sons hauled the stone from our railway station with horses and carts. The stones were pitched on end to form a foundation to receive the smaller stones. Load after load came up from the station.

Mr Spires' strawberry roan cart-horses drew the carts and the stone was tipped in handy heaps along the grass verges. It took two men to undo the pins on the 'sword' of the cart, and, after removing the tailboard, tip the cart, shooting the great stones from the breach. The sword of the cart was that upright lever-looking piece of metal where the cart shafts joined the cart body. It had holes every two inches up its length so that a pin could govern the tilt of the cart. You see, the cart body was hinged both sides near the wheels, and the sword allowed the body of the cart to tilt as the slit in the fore end slid up and down on it, but always controlled by an iron pin.

Men worked with stock axes or jadders cutting the overgrown grass and soil from the roadside. They wheeled it away and tipped their barrows forming heaps of soil at the side of the road. The steam-roller stood overnight near Mr Bailey's house at Tythe Court. Alongside the heap of steam coal a black living-van housed the one-armed driver.

As the stone from the railway trucks was levelled by hand, the great roller with its brass emblem on the front ground the stone into place. The fly-wheel spun round, smoke billowed from the tall chimney, as the driver spun the wheel which steered it. A few yards at a time it went, then chuff chuff chuff chuff and back again over the same ground.

Smaller stones were broadcast from the carts and these were pressed in, filling the crevices between the heavy ones. Then the MacAdam way of road-making followed its usual pattern as gravel, soil, sand and grit were rolled in. At this point Mr Spiers unhitched one of his horses from the cart and hooked it in between the shafts of the water-cart. He drove to the nearest ditch, threw a piece of corrugated hose into the water and pumped the handle of the cart until the barrel was full. Gingerly his horse drew the barrel of water over the new road. As the tap was turned on at the rear the water sprayed in jets from the length of horizontal pipe into the sand, the earth, grit, etc. Chuff chuff chuff came the roller and the moist mixture cemented the dry mixture into a reasonable surface. But the times the giant travelled backwards and forwards seemed endless.

In places where the road had sunk, Council workmen threw shovelfuls of grit in front of the roller, and here we would compare the old MacAdam way of road-making with the sophisticated tarmac near the station. But the station road was the beginning of the end of the method devised so long ago by that famous Scot.

CHAPTER SIXTEEN

The Village Street

The real heyday of steam had passed some years before my birth. The petrol engine, perfected as we thought then by Herbert Austin, Henry Ford and William Morris, became more common on our main roads. The village lanes were avoided and we played football uninterrupted, for an hour at a time, by cars or lorries.

I watched the steam waggons fill their tanks with water at the Turn Pike. They dropped their hoses in a ditch where the watercress grew. A ditch which never ran dry. As they pumped away, a little steam hissed from a pipe by the short funnel, steam which made the farm horses lay their ears and sometimes run away.

These steam waggons, Sentinels, Fodens, etc., usually pulled a trailer and the wheels were shod with solid rubber tyres. Woolastons of Shirley, I remember, hauled Canadian wheat from Avonmouth to Birmingham. Then Healings of Tewkesbury had a fine fleet of steam road locos. Their No. 8 was particularly fast and many was the time during the rail strike, the General Strike of 1926, when I'd been sucked along by the slip-stream of Healings No. 8 on my bicycle at twenty m.p.h.

Dad did little night-driving in his car. We walked to Chapel on a January night in 1926 to see Mr Masters of Evesham unload what was known as 'The Gold and Silver Tree', a Christmas tree loaded with bags of money towards the building expenses. Each bag contained its text or motto. One of them comes to mind: 'God loves a cheerful giver.'

We went by car to the parochial tea at Beckford. The

concert after was a Church affair with the handbell ringers included in the programme.

Reverend Harcourt Fowler left Elmley that year and was missed at these entertainments. He used the road slowly by tricycle.

It never occurred to me then that our railway line would ever be closed. A lifeline to Birmingham and the north. Bristol for the south and west.

The village street in the morning was a picture of intense industry. The cows came up from Tun Flun in the early light in spring. They followed a hurricane-lamp in the dark winter before dawn. Horses walked nose to tail, haltered on the way to the stable and breakfast. Men walked to work on the field carrying their frail baskets, their tea cans, breeched, gaitered and hobnail-shod.

Then later the postman came on his carrier bike from Evesham with the letters. The baker's cart stopped and the baker hooked the reins to a hook in the front of his covered cab.

Ladies on sit-up-and-beg cycles with dress guards rode to and from the shop, the baker and the Post Office. I watched with delight as I stood by the pub wall with Frank to see Jim Vale mount his polished Raleigh bike. He had a step on the rear hub on the near side. His left foot was placed on the step while he scooted along with his right, then when enough pace had been gathered he vaulted over the back of the saddle bag and landed on the saddle. Oh, a lot of the older men did this exercise. We learnt to mount a simpler way but that's another story.

Vans and lorries were rare in the village of my youth, the first ones being DCL Yeast *en route* to the baker, Lyon's Tea and that solid-tyred Trojan van Brooke Bond Tea to Mrs Cresswell's shop. I believe the beer at the Star came on Felton's lorry, or was it Rowlands?

To walk the road to school in an ordinary way was unusual. The village boys and girls bowled their hoops made from drill wheels, whipped their tops, leap-frogged or walked on stilts made from the ash coppice. I had a train to catch so I had to put my best foot forward to be on time. The striking thing was it was impossible to go up the road without seeing something to talk about.

Everyone's hens fetched their grit from the road. Mr Barnett's goats were gathered on the grassy banks. Mrs Cornell's goats grazed outside her house.

Some Saturday mornings, I watched our cows and kept them in bounds as they pulled the fresh green spring grass from the wider strips, the roadside, the hedge. Mr Cotton carried his candle lantern to Chapel Sunday nights and left it in the porch. He was a great walker and always seemed happy with a wheelbarrow as he went to his allotment during the summer evenings. I must mention here that he once built a miniature wheat rick complete with staddle and thatched for the Harvest Festival. It was so much admired that a piece was in the local paper about it.

Just after Harvest Festival that year Frank and I biked to Evesham to the Mop, saw a horse with five legs and pinched the fat lady in a tent outside the Star Hotel for threepence.

Dad did use his car later that year one night when Mother tempted him out to go to Evesham to hear Mark Hambourg, the famous pianist. I stayed in. Bach, Chopin, Beethoven and Mozart just didn't appeal.

It is a thought that for generations the roads have been a meeting place in the village. You see when the water was fetched from the standpipe or pump, people did make conversation. It is true some roads are much older than others, but after a day behind the plough or harrow when the clay clung to the boots, I've seen men going home. Going home scuffing their boots on the road, always carrying some thing, a scythe, a hedge hook, a hoe. I remember Ralph Davis, after he had taken a dray-load of fruit to market, walking past our house carrying a log for the fire. The folk who walked to and from work then seemed duty bound to take home a good hawthorn log from the hedge bottom where they had worked, or a rabbit caught by a dog, or (who knows) a wire snare.

Some have said, 'It's a lonely road.'

I saw a busy road not of motor traffic but people, animals, to and fro from morning until night.

The green fields are a good place to be in summer, but even then the hard road to the cottage door and tea-time is a happy place.

CHAPTER SEVENTEEN

Pigs, Horses, Goats, Sheep

That's what Prince Henry's Grammar School was called when I first stepped into the cloakroom in September 1926 with number 1132 on my goods and chattels.

Miss Morris gave me a good report and a heavy Bible when I left her delightful school in July of that year.

In this age of self-expression, PHGS was an alien world. The folk who expressed were few. Two in fact – the product of Durham University, Dr S. Rennie Hazelhurst, and Mrs Knight-Coutts. I'll be bold enough to say that not only the pupils but the rest of the staff were afraid of these two Heads. I imagine that the Governors themselves bowed low to the man from the north. Discipline. Don't make me laugh.

To be fair, I gather that the school had sunk to a low ebb before the doctor's arrival. It's easy to describe him because I've never met another man like him before or since. He stalked the hall in chalk-smothered gown, burnt in holes with acid from the chemistry laboratory. At times he wore a mortar-board over his receding grey hair. His grey suit, including the waistcoat, was riddled with acid burns. When I arrived I was drafted into Miss Lambshead's class and I steered clear of him for a time except at morning prayers or assembly. More like sabre rattling. Here I learnt that 'some can pot begonias, others bud a rose, and some are hardly fit to be with anything that grows'.

The Doc was such an overwhelming figure that the rest of the staff, who were, I suppose, good for their time, have almost vanished into oblivion.

Prefects were encouraged in a form of sadism I had never known before. To be bumped, ducked and slippered as a new boy by these swaggering bullies, some of whom had started to shave, was looked upon by the Doc as 'taking your medicine'.

How we applauded Wally, that sturdy fourteen-year-old son of a cider maker, when three of his House leaders went to fetch him from the cloakroom. Wally had endured too many detentions which, of course, went against his House points. Wally invited them to fetch him and then the bombardment of football boots followed as he slung them at the hobbledehoys. Wally was not slippered but a young lad of my age from Pershore was. Son of a widowed mother of the First World War, a special scholarship boy who went home that night with half a shirt. Why, I ask, should anyone cover up the glass-house atmosphere of Prince Henry's of 1926?

The Doc practised caning of whole classes or forms for the misdemeanour of one boy. I had no hesitation in summing him up as a sadist.

I remember the kindness of George Sutton; of ex-army officer James Tate who taught Latin and Mr Carter, sports master. These three behaved like grown men and treated us like growing men. As for the rest of the staff, indoctrinated by the doctor, they took pleasure in giving open-handed blows to the ear and knocking us across the desks.

I suppose what really riled me about the Head was when he caned Hanks. I was sitting by Hanks one morning when Miss Lambshead had left the class room for a few minutes, and a girl prefect in charge of us said, 'Quiet, all of you, the Doctor's in the hall.'

'I don't care, let him stop there,' said Hanks. This was passed on to the graduate of Durham and all the boys were filed into the hall.

'Touch your toes, boy,' Hazelhurst bawled out. Then the bamboo swished and stung Hanks' backside where his grey flannel shorts reached to his thighs. The Doc flailed away at him for what must have been ten to fifteen minutes until the weals left by the cane handle were raised into fiery red half-moons on his naked thighs. Hanks squealed like a benched pig, imploring the Doc to stop, but in vain. We went back to our desks cowed, disgusted, sorry for Hanks who had recently lost his mother.

I knew there were certain limits to punishment in those days. I also knew Superintendent Pass who shot over our land. A council of war was called and five of us volunteered to take Hanks and show the Super what had been done. But Hanks was afraid to go. I think it was because of his father.

From that day, at eleven years old, when I had only been at the Grammar School a short time, I felt no respect for the Doctor. Only fear. It affected my lessons in such a way that to walk across the hall from one class room to another was to walk in fear, always expecting a forefinger to be bent and a voice to boom out, 'Boy, come here.'

To say that every minute of school was torment would be an over-statement. Nature walks with Miss Lambshead by the riverside and stories of Japan from Mr Sharp when he should have been teaching double entry book-keeping were a respite.

Then a school orchestra was formed. They played two tunes at school parties, 'There ain't no sense sitting on a fence all by yourself in the moonlight', and 'I never tasted kisses until the other night, how long has this been going on?'

Not much of a dancer, I did feel a fool when I chose for my partner the wife of a junior master. She was skittish and looking like a fifth former. I remember asking her if she was sitting for the School Cert. that year!

Speech days, when every year, Alderman Felton, one of the Governors, told us he was the oldest boy as he stood on the platform. Sir Edward Elgar came once and the choir sang a piece set to his music to please him.

I know we boys who travelled to school on the Ashchurch train deserved all we got as we slung the sticks from the railway carriage blinds when our little tank engine pulled the three coaches over the river bridge and dropped them into the Avon. Little did we know the guard could see us in that slit of a window up the length of the train from his van. So, in impressive braid, the station master of Evesham came with the guard and they told their story to the Doctor as we sat in a little circle in his office.

The thing which to this day baffles me is that when I used my season ticket on a Saturday morning to fetch Mr Bailey's and Dad's market money, if any member of the staff saw me hatless, this was reported to the Head and I could be sure of four strokes of the bamboo rod on Monday morning.

We used to put our pennies in the slot machine and got one Churchmans No. 1 wrapped in foil and guaranteed to last fifteen minutes which was the exact time our homeward train took to reach Ashton station. This would have meant twelve strokes of the cane had the Doc known. But he knew too much already.

CHAPTER EIGHTEEN

Eclipse of the Sun

Even at eleven years old I had seen the black clouds of thunder blot out the sun and the candles lit in our kitchen in the middle of the day. But the morning of June 29th 1927, was going to be different. At school it was explained to us that on that morning soon after sunrise the moon would for a short while be between us on earth and the sun. Darkness would fall again on earth after the dawn.

Mr Cave told us it would be his last chance to see such a spectacle. 1999 would be the next year this would happen.

'Nineteen-ninety-nine,' I thought. 'That will make me eighty-four and the Bible only makes life span out for seventy years. I'll have been on trespass here for fourteen years.'

It was nothing for Mr Cave to get up at three o'clock in the morning. He liked to read his Bible in the small hours when his mind was clear.

He advised us boys to get up before dawn and watch the eclipse. Oh yes, we were warned at school of the danger of looking at the sun with naked eyes as it could cause harm to our eyesight. Smoked glasses were advisable or even half a brown beer bottle.

John and Tom and I made ready for that morning trip up Bredon Hill days before the event. We used long-wick candles to smoke plain pieces of glass to use as scanners on that June morning. Mr Cave and John walked to our house well before dawn and we joined them. The disturbed dogs barked as we passed the Post Office. It was cold. The dew soaked our boots and under the stars the village slept.

Up through the Close gateway and over the stile the footpath took us past the ghostly outline of pollard elms when we arrived at the foot of Little Hill.

'No need to climb to Bredon's summit,' Mr Cave said, 'but just high enough to be above the village and the trees where the line of the Cotswold Edge will be plain.'

'It's the Cuckoo Pen then,' I said, and thought that a few yards below that clump of beeches on the brow of the hill, an outcrop of limestone formed a perfect seat, just a shallow cliff three feet high. But we were too late. A knot of villagers were sitting there, Creef, a great lover of nature and the hill, among them.

A bank of cloud lay like a blanket over the stars towards Cleeve Hill. It moved towards Evesham Vale. What a pity, we all thought, after being so clear a sky. But the golden rays of the sun did peep over the Cotswold Edge like a glow of distant fire.

There was nothing between us on Bredon and the formation of limestone which stretches from Meon Hill near Stratford-upon-Avon almost to Bath. Just the Evesham Vale and the Vale of Gloucester.

Quite near Broadway Tower the sun rose a little more, lighting up once again the hundreds of thousands or even millions of years old Cotswolds, bastions to the Vale.

I had seen better sunrises. The clouds blew like smoke across its golden face. Then the birds were singing. The quice or wood-pigeon called, 'My toe bleeds, Betty' from the pollard elms at the bottom of Little Hill. Blackbirds called in the thorn hedge of Paris Hill. Young rabbits ventured from their holes under the gorse. Ashton's farmyard cocks crew and we saw the smoke of wood and coal rise from the cottage chimneys.

It was eerie at the Cuckoo Pen. No one spoke.

'No, it isn't the end of the world,' I thought, 'because then the moon turns to blood.'

The moon hung like a big silver Catherine wheel among the clouds.

Then it was as if some wondrous plan schemed out ages ago came to fruition.

The rising sun – what a shame the clouds were spoiling it! – approached the moon.

I knew the sun lay millions of miles behind the moon, but how exciting to think that just for once in a lifetime the moon would completely blot out its light to us.

As the top half of the sun was darkened we looked with amazement. It was as if the moon had planned to show us its place in the expanse of space around.

One old man who had climbed the hill that day before going to work in the fields wondered how the papers and the wireless knew it was going to happen on June 29.

From twilight to almost inky darkness seemed only a matter of seconds.

The sun was eclipsed by the moon.

The birds went back to roost. The skylark grounded once more and as we stood there I thought once more of the miracles of the Bible. The darkness of Calvary.

'Glasses ready,' said Mr Cave as a hair's breadth of sickled sunshine peeped through the clouds behind the moon.

There was really no need for smoked glasses, the clouds took the brightness away. The sickled light grew until it became a golden crown.

When half the sun appeared again the birds sang once more. The smoke showed grey from the cottage chimneys hundreds of feet below.

A broken-voiced cuckoo called late from Mr Nicklin's orchard and the jays and magpies squawked in the Primrose Coppice. As I walked home down Church Close by the Moat and through the churchyard while the men went to their work, the smell of fried bacon met me at the door. Dad had the hoop-handled frying pan slung from the pot-hook.

'Nineteen-ninety-nine,' I thought, 'no need to worry about that. That's a lifetime away.'

Yes, it was a lifetime away. And what is a lifetime? 'Three score years and ten,' Mr Cotton said at Sunday School.

Yet a lifetime in comparison with the workings of earth, sun, moon and stars – well it's just a fleeting moment.

One tick of a watch would be to exaggerate it.

A falling leaf describes it.

CHAPTER NINETEEN

School Leaver

From twelve years old we were expected to wear a black coat and waistcoat with pin-striped trousers for Chapel on Sundays and important days at school. The starched shirt collars added to the agony of those days. I don't think growing boys were ever intended to be fenced in around the neck by such a contraption.

It was also a contortion for me to fasten the back stud. Still, that was the pattern and we roamed the village streets and fields as if we had escaped from Eton.

I want to forget school for obvious reasons so will just be brief about my last day there. Due partly to illness, partly to laziness, I fell sadly behind with lessons, being absent so often. Christmas approached and I pleaded with Dad to get my discharge. The School Certificate was on the June horizon and it was obvious that my name was never going to be in gold leaf on the school wall for any special achievement.

The Doc had four of us leavers in his office on the last day. He sat there in his mortar-board and gown with his feet on the mantelpiece, and warned us against wine and women. Quite unnecessary but ritual. Then he said, 'Archer, what are you going to do?'

'A farmer, sir,' I said, calling him 'sir' for the last time.

'Um,' came the retort. 'You will have to farm with your feet. You've no brains.'

Then as the smoke from his black ebony-looking pipe filled the room he told us not to smoke. 'Why do I smoke my pipe?' he asked one of us.

'Don't know sir,' he said.

'Habit,' said the Doc. 'Don't get into bad habits,' adding, 'I smoke my pipe for the same reason as I wear my boots.'

Never has music sounded so sweet as on that breaking-up day when we sang 'Lord dismiss us with thy blessing'.

It was over. Over for good.

The royal-blue school uniform which had matched the school magazine was thrown aside as soon as I had saved enough money to buy clothes which I thought fit for the country.

The shops closed late on Saturday nights and I was determined to look like an under-carter, shepherd or cowman. The Bedford Cord breeches with leather strapping, smelt a bit for a time and Mother said the grey tweed jacket with a poacher's pocket big enough to hold two rabbits looked like those worn by inmates of the Workhouse. Still, cousin Tom, who had rolled his puttees scores of times when he was in the Worcesters, showed me how to put mine on to complete the outfit. Plough and Harrow brand boots from Wylies were waterproof, but oh they were heavy after the school Uskhide type!

'I suppose you'd better help Tom Whittle with the cattle,' Dad said. 'He's got a lot to fodder on the hill and the calves to rear.'

Just to be with Tom and help him load the kerves of hay into the muck cart as Turpin stood in the shafts by the side of the rick was very satisfying. We fed the out-wintered stores, all heifers, all dark red Herefords with hay on the frozen hill. Then Tom carried a sack of kibbled cake from Great Hill Barn and put a few pounds into each feeding tub, feeding tubs made of small half-barrels by Jack Hunting. I often thought of Tom when the snow covered the thatch of the hay rick and he stripped off the icy straw and pulled out the rick pegs for me to stack in a heap under the wall. He would stop for a minute and breathe the warm air from his moustache-capped mouth into his numb fingers. 'Allus the same when I have to start another cut on the rick,' he said. 'Either snowing, freezing or blowing a gale.' When the straw was off and Tom climbed the ladder carrying the cutting-knife to guillotine the hay into square kerves like pressed mattresses of sweet-smelling fodder, he threw the first burden down for me to stack on to the cart.

The heifers bawled over the gate, waiting for breakfast, dinner and tea all in one. As the knife cut through the hay by the sheer weight and strength of Tom's bent body, the rick stood like a cake on a tea table. A cake sliced straight and even by Aunty Polly. Why did the hay cutters be so particular about keeping straight? A pride in their work. No other reason. The rick lasted no longer for it.

As I led Turpin with the cart-load of fodder across the flat of Spring Hill, Tom scattered the hay in a straight line as he shuppicked or pitch-forked it from the tail of the cart. The heifers followed us and after a couple of Rugby scrums as they hooved each other for the best position in the line-up, they settled down to feed on the honey-scented cured grass of the previous June. This was the boy I wanted to be. Working with Tom. Listening to his experiences of winters long ago. Drinking in every word and wondering how he knew so much of life in general and why he was so content with his lot.

Those happy days on the hill were better still when I rode Kitty, the little mare which Dad bought me for a pound a leg at Candlemas Fair. We left Turpin after he had eaten his ration of oats to feed with the heifers on the hill.

Some winter days the snow lay in the gullies which the cart had made and everywhere looked the same as the weak rays of the wintry sun shone on the scene. Tom would simply say, 'White world this morning, Fred bwoy.' Nothing of interest could be seen but the patterns of rabbits' feet, hares' feet and foxes' feet – tracks in the snow which told tales of the previous night. Told us where they went to earth or form. The twittering of skylarks and the plaintive call of peewits in the spring were a promise of better weather to come. Nature worked very slow but very sure.

In that first spring of working regularly on the land, Ralph had ploughed the Thurness late. It must have been March when the clay furrows folded over like yellow liver. The cold winds set the land like cement and the needed frost never came. Mr Bailey and Dad looked it over one evening and saw the tell-tale shoots of squitch grass or couch grass green between the ploughing.

'Better plough it back again, Tom,' Mr Bailey said.

Next morning, at seven, Ralph and I, with four horses hooked or hitched on to the Kell plough, started ploughing back.

That land was like concrete, and as I walked up and down, stumbling over the clats or clods, holding the traces to keep me on an even keel, I thought perhaps Dad was right when he suggested I should have trained to be a parson? Why a parson? You may well ask. One reason, the only reason I heard, was that I cared very little for what people said about me. Learning English at Grammar School was of little use in ploughing back the Thurness. Thurness means a giant's nose and that was the shape of the field.

'Ett,' shouted Ralph when Boxer or Turpin left the furrow and walked on the unploughed land. 'Awr,' he called as the horses went too far over on the ploughing. But on the addledum or headland the commands were not unlike those of a military manoeuvre. 'Turn come agun' or 'Come agun', Ralph said if we were casting a bed of land or turning to the left. 'Turn jinkum' or 'Jig agun' if we were ridging a land or turning right.

Then as Captain, the filler at the back, ran off so that the plough came out I heard, 'Comey back awr' or 'Gee back' and 'ett' if the four horses needed pushing off to the right.

But this was the English I enjoyed. Shakespeare under Bredon Hill.

Our team of foremost lash horse, body horse and filler were exactly like the teams of a hundred years ago. Shakespeare had spoken of the fill horse or filler when in *The Merchant of Venice* he wrote of Old Gobbo, 'Thou hast got more hair on thy chin than Dobbin my Fill-horse has on his tail.'

I could write volumes about Ralph. But suffice it to say what interest and energy he put into his work. How he loved to see the day shine in the morning sun as the upturned furrow exposed the worms to the rooks. How he hated the ploughing to muffle or moot when the earth clung to the shieldboard and had to be scraped off with the paddle or little spade on the headland.

I learnt a lot from Ralph. The determined plodding behind the plough as work went on day in, day out.

To think of the days before the horses went off the land makes music of jingling harness.

It amused me to think how, compared with the depth of coal mines, tin mines, we on the land just scratched at the world's surface. Six inches was a fair depth for horse ploughing. Ten inches the tractor plough penetrated. Then the steam cultivator often brought up clats or clods of earth from eighteen inches down. Messrs Bomford Bros., that inventive family who pioneered farm mechanisation, came along with a revolutionary idea the gyrotiller. A monster on tracks, which stirred the soil two feet deep and sometimes stirred the shallow drains. This machine, viewed with suspicion by the older worker, was soon accepted.

'I look at it like this,' Ralph said. 'It breaks the pan, allows the water to drain away in the winter, stirs the ground without bringing the mast [subsoil] to the top.'

The gyrotiller usually came in August driven by Bert Wright, a wizard with agricultural machinery.

I was more involved in skimming. The skim or shim plough invented by engineers like Burlingham of Evesham, Larkworthy of Worcester, did exactly what it says, skim the surface. The rectangular frame with two handles like plough handles had two feet, one on each side. These feet bolted to the legs which were bolted to the frame. The feet each had a share. The shares were iron blades, the cutting edge hammered sharp on the blacksmith's anvil cut the weeds. The two shares formed a letter V which almost met. In fact the gap was about two inches, a gap necessary for the cut weeds to filter through. The depth of skimming was determined by the set of the wheels. Two wheels at the front on stems and axles held to the frame by iron collars. Oh yes, the simple tackle.

One spanner fitted everything and even the spanner was made at Tom Higgins', the local blacksmith.

With the one-horse skim and George holding the tails, or handles, and me guiding the horse through the endless rows of sprouts, we walked many miles a day. When the sun shone the weeds withered.

Before I had left school I had seen, so often, Mr Bailey and Dad pulling a wooden hand-marker to mark out the rows for the sprout plants. Just a wooden frame with legs formed by the rounds, or rungs, from an old ladder, and the ladder side was the tool bar. In those days sprouts were planted three feet between the rows, but the distance between the plants varied according to the man with the setting pins or dibber. He may have set his plants two feet six inches apart in the row or two feet nine inches.

Now the local sprout growers had a good ally in Tom Higgins. Tom was a blacksmith with an inventive mind. A bit of prompting and suggestion from a grower and Tom would make anything.

I'm not going to explain the steerage horse-hoe, except that it had a tool bar where the legs and shears could be adjusted according to the width between the rows of crops. Tom made a long tool bar to replace the usual one for marking out. Five legs it had, fixed with collars and set screws, so by placing these three feet apart and running the one leg down the last mark, four marks could be made for sprout planting.

Now we come to a change of pattern in sprout growing. By marking a field lengthways, and crossways, and planting the sprouts where the two lines met or on the square, the sprouts could be skimmed or horse-hoed both ways. This saved a lot of work, because the only part left for hand-hoeing was the small square of ground around the plant where the skim didn't cut the weeds. So George and I scratched the top two inches of soil day after day; a continual battle with chickweed, groundsel, coltsfoot, sow thistles, which we cut below ground level and kept the mould or tilth moving about every three weeks through the summer. Then we had the two-horse skim which

Ralph used with horses abreast, cleaning ground after the pea crop. This implement was in constant use in the plum plantation cleaning the land between the alleyways of trees. A tandem job with two of us boys leading foremost and filler horse, and the nearer we could get to the trees the less hand-work for the men hoeing.

What a caper this was! It was a job we dreaded. Ralph dreaded it too. I almost felt the horses dreaded it. The branches of plum trees in early summer, already bowed down with green marbles of plums, were our trouble.

As we slaughtered the ever-growing pelf rait, as Ralph and George called every weed, thistles scored Geoff's legs and my legs leading the horses through what was often a jungle in the Vale. George and Ralph said they wouldn't be surprised if some wild animal came out of the undergrowth. But nothing worse than wasps' nests plagued us, then it was hold tight to the horses.

Mr Bailey and Dad kept an eye on us and came daily, breeched and gaitered, through the gate by the hovel where we had our bait, or lunch. Dad's clearing of his throat gave us the cue above the jingling harness that they had arrived. As the weeds were thick the skim reaved or choked and, every so often, Ralph shouted 'Whoa', as he lifted the skim handles above his head leaving a heap of weeds before we went on again. 'Can you get a bit closer to the trees?' Dad said.

'Ett ett,' Ralph called to Geoff and me and the tops of the horses' hames peeled the bark from the overhanging plum boughs.

'Look, Tom, they ull ruin the trees,' Mr Bailey said. 'I'd rather them not get so close.'

'But what a lot there will be left to hoe, Harry,' Dad said.

Ralph mopped his brow, Geoff and I said nothing, then Ralph said, 'You be the man as pays Friday night, but you can't have it all roads. I can't skim anant [close to] the trees without barking some of the branches.'

Mr Bailey and Dad pondered, looked at the weeds, looked at the sap browning from the torn bark. They went to Tom

Higgins. As they went, I remember Ralph saying to Mr Bailey, 'It's collars we want for the osses without any hames to rip the trees about.'

'Breast collars do you mean, Ralph?' Mr Bailey said.

'Oi, that's it.'

Down at Sedgeberrow, Archer and Bailey and Tom Higgins thought out a plan to skim near to the plum trees. A long share to run two feet wider than the skim frame would cut the weeds under the trees without Geoff and me leading our horses too close and ripping the trees about with the hames. Hames which stood up above the horse-collars like raised arms as village folk voted at the parish meeting.

The shear was fitted and Ralph said, 'Now then, you boys, don't let the hames mark the trees. Keep far enough away from overhanging boughs.' Off we went, but sometimes Ralph called 'Ett' or pushed the horse closer to the row and the one hame would catch an overhanging Prolific tree. (They were the worst.) The skim would peel off the bough. Ralph called, 'Whoa, what did I tell ya.' Where the bark had peeled we rubbed some soil to make it less obvious, but Ralph said, 'I'll bet them men as pays ull spot it when they come tomorrow happen.'

CHAPTER TWENTY

Village Politics and the Depression

I suppose we Vale folk, who in winter took clay home on hobnailed boots, have been thought of as the parish pump politicians. It's true we were parochial. Dad talked at home almost in fear and trembling about the prospect of ever being ruled from Whitehall. There is a continuity in village life. It's a life which hates change.

Dr Roberson had been our Councillor for much longer than I could remember. He had served the village well on parish council, rural district council and every other council, except the County council. Through deafness and age, the time came for him to retire. I think deafness was his chief handicap because, as Chairman of the Pebworth Rural District Council, he often was unable to keep pace with the business and asked for a proposer and seconder of a motion after it had been passed. He had served his time and an election was arranged for the parish council. Dad took his place on that. But in our village it's true to say that, thank God, the ordinary people were not a lot of yes men. It's true some lived in tied cottages, cottages which went with their jobs. Cottagers were then beholden to their employers.

After the parish election, Pedlar from Paris and some of his fellow travellers were not satisfied with the result. In fact they said it was a kind of frame up.

One Sunday morning, after Dad had been nominated for the rural district council, the village was plastered with printed posters. Some were not at all complimentary to the rulers of the village. I remember one which said, 'Beware of the wolf in sheep's clothing. They have had you over the parish council, don't let them have you over the district council.' Folk going to Church and Chapel on Sunday were flabbergasted at a poem about one of Ashton's leaders. The name he was given had never been associated with him before, and the printer omitted to print his own name at the foot of the poster. That week, as the black and white messages of dissatisfaction hung drawing-pinned from elm trees, on make-shift notice boards and on one man's front door, the whole place buzzed with speculation.

Solicitor's opinion was that the parish pump politicians had just kept within the law. Oh, the printer was in error but no action was taken.

And so, with a stormy beginning, Dad succeeded Dr Roberson as village member on the RDC and member of the Guardians Committee.

Even then there was a need for council houses for the village and soon a plot was found at the Elmley Road, and a local builder built our first eight houses. The rent for these, including rates, was about four shillings a week. And so the village grew with me.

I thought then how grand the houses were compared with the thatched hovels the landworkers had lived in. It's so true that black and white thatch cottages, however pretty on postcards, are grim inside before modernisation. Condemned as unfit for human habitation, the black and white of our village stood as empty sepulchres for more years than I care to think.

I suppose the first big decision Dad had to make came a little later on the council agenda. More houses had been built, still at a rent the farm worker and his wife could pay by thrift and good management. A few of these houses, however, were allocated to families a notch higher in the social scale. Better off than the twenty-nine shillings and threepenny men on the land. I heard of men getting two pounds ten shillings a week in Evesham.

These people were not content to carry drinking water from

the standpipe taps of the village street. It had been such a familiar sight, something I had thought inevitable that men should carry buckets of water and place them under the tapless crock sink.

A couple of new private houses went up and were connected to the council main. The two pounds ten a week men wanted to be connected to the village water supply, but the pressure in the pipes was too low and the RDC could do nothing, as the council houses stood at the highest point in the village.

All the water came from Paris on the Hill, but from three reservoirs. The council main was a second-hand Cheltenham gas-pipe, sixty years old. The Deacle Charity Supply. This fed the houses on the estate and our supply, which provided water for our farm, Mr Bailey's and the Cross Cottages. There were various wells still being used, but Paris was the place oozing with water. Water enough to supply several villages, but not high enough up the hill to push it to the council houses themselves. So the ball-taps fizzed and burped in the tanks at the roadside outside the new houses, filling up at night when the village slept and no one drew water lower down the street.

Householders are entitled to attend and vote at parish meetings. I, in my late teens, was allowed to attend but not vote. Curious and anxious, I went to the school to an extraordinary parish meeting called by the fifty shillings a week men who wanted a new village main water supply, so that the taps would run over their sinks. You couldn't blame them; we, and more like us, had water in the house lower down the village. Dad listened to the pros and cons, listened to the surveyor's opinion. In those days there was no load spreading. The householder who wanted the water would have to pay for the new main pipe. Others opted out. The noisy, unruly meeting, chaired admirably by William Baldwyn, was told by the surveyor that a connection could be made to the main pipe at the next village, but the council house rent and rates would be increased by at least half-a-crown a week to pay for it.

Dad said at that meeting that the houses were built for the

landworkers and he wanted their opinion. As one man, they said that half-a-crown a week was more than they could afford and they were satisfied.

Mr Jim Cotton did say, and right he was, that we had lots of water higher up the hill than Paris, but the surveyor was not interested. This water would have supplied the top of the village, independent of the council main. Isn't that what we wanted, to be independent?

That evening, as Dad sided with the low-paid landworkers, he found for the first time that he had offended some of the tenants. I was proud of Dad. He didn't forget the old days when his parents had to scrape a living, when if his crippled mother's cat strayed after rabbits in the adjoining field, it would be shot.

Many families that night stood on the bottom rung of life's ladder. They climbed it step by step. Men carried the water from the roadside taps, but they paid their rent. Parish politics, you may say; Whitehall was feared.

It was when Dad was appointed Guardian of the Poor of our village that I first became deeply interested in that side of life, more especially workhouses. Why workhouses? Because seeing villagers go to these institutions gave me the feeling that people were being buried alive.

A man who sits, aged and drooling, on a grassy bank of a village street is in much more natural surroundings than in the carbolic prison house of an institution. I had learnt at school Crabbe's description of the workhouses of his time:

There in yon house that holds the Parish Poor,
Whose walls of mud scarce hold the broken door.
There where the putrid vapours flagging play
And the dull wheel hums doleful through the day,
There children dwell who know no parents' care.
Heart-broken maidens on their joyless bed,
Forsaken wives and mothers never wed
Dejected widows with unheeded tears,
And crippled age with more than childhood fears,

The lame, the blind, and far the happiest they,
The Moping Idiot and the madman gay.

I suppose almost every village then had its poorhouse supported by the parish rate. I had spoken to one man who had experienced the treadmill of a jailhouse and understood Crabbe's mood as he said, 'And the dull wheel hums doleful all the day.'

But the Poor Law had changed before my youth. Union workhouses catered for the poor of several parishes. Evesham had a Union Poor Law Institution, 'The Grubber' as it was called.

The Union Workhouse had a casual ward where tramps, travellers, stayed one night, had breakfast and were given a meal ticket, so that if they were walking to Tewkesbury or Cheltenham after their allotted task of work, they called at Beckford, exchanging the ticket for a slice of bread and cheese and a little tea. I do recollect that the permanent inmates, if married, met only in the gardens. The men worked in the gardens and fed the pigs with the swill from the kitchen. The women did housework. 'Whom God had joined together, let no man put asunder' didn't apply to the Poor Law. Yes, old folk feared the workhouse.

As we were in Gloucestershire and always had been in the Rural District of Pebworth, the Hundred of Tibalstone, Evesham was in a different county – Worcestershire.

Men and women of Ashton who became aged and infirm had been accepted at Evesham Union Workhouse without question. It must have been about 1928 when some genius of local government decided that Gloucestershire people from Ashton-under-Hill and Aston Somerville were being kept by Worcestershire rates.

Spider and Nathan, two Ashton men who had lived their lives on the land and slept in farmhouse bothies and outbuildings of the Star Inn, became unable to look after themselves. They went to Evesham Union Workhouse. Spider was happy in the gardens among the cabbages. Nathan fed the pigs.

After one meeting of the Board of Guardians, Dad and Lady Norah Fitzherbert found that the Gloucestershire men had been moved to Cheltenham. Lady Norah, being the representative for Aston Somerville visited Cheltenham Workhouse. Nothing wrong with Cheltenham Workhouse, but she found the men from the two parishes very unhappy. 'You see, ma'am,' Nathan told her, 'I allus looked upon the pigs at A'sum Workhouse as my charges.'

'Mr Archer, we must do something,' she told Dad. 'These men are heart-broken.'

I suppose to a certain extent it was not unusual for Dad to take the law into his own hands. He made a man who had stolen his bike off the main road work for him for a week. He fed him, sent him on his way to Cardiff. Dad spoke to the Cheltenham Workhouse Master, who told him that he could release the men as casuals or vagrants and send them to Evesham. The Evesham Workhouse Master agreed to accept them (he had to). So one morning during the Easter Holiday, Dad drove the Sunbeam to the outskirts of Cheltenham and picked up four men walking the Evesham Road. They solemnly got in the car and came to our house. Mother had mugs of cocoa and bread, cheese and onions, and here I saw these men around our scrubbed kitchen table, as Dad put it, 'Just like schoolboys coming home on holiday.' He took them on to Evesham Casual Ward. I have reason to believe the good Master at Evesham gave them back their places among their friends.

The next Guardians' Meeting was stormy, as Lady Norah and Dad, who had flouted officialdom, had to explain the situation. The Guardians allowed them to stay and three years later we were transferred to Worcestershire, so the problem never arose again.

You have no idea how proud I was of Dad on the day Spider and Nathan came back, but had he studied the parish records, as I have done since, his case for their admission to Evesham Union would have been undisputed.

To quote: 'It was decided at Ashton Vestry Meeting in 1860 to sell 8 cottages to raise money for Evesham Union.'

Then again: 'April 20th, 1870. Application made to Poor
Law Board for permission to draw certain money belonging to
the Parish now lying in funds for the purpose of defraying part
of the expenses falling on this Parish incurred in erecting new
buildings for a hospital at Evesham Union House Hampton.'

Why were Spider and Nathan sent to Cheltenham after our
village helped to build Evesham Union? I wonder. Did the
bureaucrats walk by on the other side of the road?

Lady Norah and Dad didn't, thank God.

You will notice that my interest in local affairs, after the
Union affair, became more intense.

It's not my intention to compare the Poor Law with the
present system of Social Security. However, I will deal briefly
with this.

I have noticed during my lifetime a distinct tendency to put
in institutions all who, through no fault of their own, are
incapable of a full day's work.

We went through a similar drastic phase in medicine. The
doctor of the '20s and '30s who saw bad teeth in his patient
sent him to the dentist to have them all out. Poison to the
system it was considered. Now things have changed and so has
the idea of institutionalisation. 'Be it ever so humble, there's
no place like home', the song goes.

Institutions there must be, but consider the gipsies. Notice
their children, how they bloom with health. Pauper is an
old-fashioned word. In the last century there were indoor and
outdoor paupers, the indoor ones living in the workhouse, while
houses were set aside for outdoor paupers. These houses were
owned by the Church and controlled by the vestry meeting.

As Guardian, Dad, who had lived in our village all his life,
knew the people pretty well. One February day, I went with
him to see Bill Allen, aged and crippled with rheumatism.
Bill, or Blenheim as he was called, had worked his life away on
the land until he was unable to crop the hedges, dig the
ditches of the farms. His pension of ten shillings per week was
not sufficient to keep body and soul together. He, more than
anyone, was entitled to some relief.

'Come with me, Bill,' Dad said, 'and see the Relieving Officer.'

After some persuasion he got in the car.

'I beunt a gwain on the Parish mind, Master Archer,' he told Dad. 'I don't fancy being beholden to nobody.'

Dad said, 'I understand, Bill, but it's different now. The Relieving Officer will be sympathetic to your case.'

You see, if a man and his wife lived together they could just manage on one pound per week, but with Bill being a bachelor it was different.

Bill put on his dark overcoat, the one, I fancy, he had worn to carry the coffin at funerals when one of his generation passed on. He went to Evesham and of course he was given a few shillings to tide him over. A good sort was Bill, for when the weather took up, he was back in the fields hoeing the peas and sprouts of the village. When he died the next year, he had saved enough in a stocking to pay for his funeral. No, Bill didn't want to be beholden to the parish.

It's a heartening thought how much pride and independence such men had, and how much they appreciated dying in their own beds after a lifetime of sunshine and storm under the thatch.

Other cases Dad dealt with as Guardian included a war widow and her large family, three of whom died of consumption. A sad case of a man who sacrificed all for his country. His widow had been brought up as a lady and her life after the war was a struggle. These are human stories of the poor of the parish.

Guardians – well, they are all gone, but they knew the needs of the people. How genuine these were! I only remember one case of a man applying for relief who had, through thrift, a good bank account. Dad knew and he had a word in his ear and the man withdrew his claim.

I suppose a lot can be said for confidential officialdom, but local knowledge of men on the spot is, or should be, a humane way of dealing with local problems. So Dad and the other Guardians were men of their time. They fulfilled a need and, being in touch, I think did a good job during the years when village folk had to count every copper.

I well remember the smell of cow manure on Harry Flute's boots as he sat in our kitchen while Dad filled in his pension form. Harry's bristly chin, his cidery breath, his chuckle when he said, 'I be no scollard, Master.'

Never having known hunger myself, I mixed and talked with men who had. 'Give us this day our daily bread', meant something to them. Bread to them was sacred. To waste a crust was a crime. It seems a long while ago.

A teenager like me (that word wasn't coined then) knew little of high finance, how the Wall Street crash spread like the eddies on a pond, as if someone had thrown a stone and ripples on the water covered the western world. I saw in the *Chronicle* pictures of the dole queues. The means test didn't really convey anything. I thought the Government was to blame. Reading of the formation of the National Government with men like J.A. Thomas, Philip Snowden, who was always in pain, throwing in their lot with Ramsay MacDonald and the Tories and some Liberals gave a sense of unity to the problems of that time.

The fact that within just over half a mile of our village, the wrecks of humanity trudged from workhouse to workhouse appeared unavoidable to me. I failed to realise then that this sore would fester for decades, but the total unfairness of the system must have been in the thoughts of my elders, more especially those who had been through the hell of total war.

The miners were out of work in South Wales. Our leeks were no longer wanted for Cardiff Market. A wholesaler from there went broke. Well, this was one of the hazards of market gardening that had been accepted by Evesham Vale.

But lambs became almost unsaleable and cattle prices got so low that many tenant farmers just couldn't find the rent for the farms. High up on Bredon, 'on the flat' as we called it, where the barn and the beeches were, a local estate made overtures for about a hundred acres or more of land. Sheep walks, rough grazings, two fields of arable.

Mr Bailey and Dad had unsuccessfully tried to find water on Spring Hill. The income for this to supply Pershore would have tided them over the depression. At last I went with Mr Bailey and Jack Hunting to get what rabbits we could off this hilltop. Then it was sold at market price and market price was low. Mr Bailey said, 'They will have it'; meaning of course that the workmen would have the money from the sale of the land. I always thought it a sad blow to Mr Bailey, who combed the land with his gun and rabbit wires, when the land on the top went.

I fetched a truck-load of wire nettings and stakes from the station and Quar Hill, a hill lower down, was wired against rabbits. The wire had to be sunk a foot in the ground to keep the rabbits out. Fred on the Fordson ploughed the virgin turf in the autumn and A and B planted the field on March 17 with runner beans. Mr Baldwyn said the 17th was the day for early runners.

Quar Hill was above the line where early spring frosts kill the crops. The soil was friable. The beans came up early in rows, then something happened we had never seen before. The rooks pulled them up. Rooks pulling up runner beans puzzled even the old shepherd. Ralph said he had never seen 'a job like that afore'. Every bean under the soil wriggled with wire worms from the cold turf. The field was planted again, but the crop was later. The next year it was planted with sprouts and what a crop! They grew all the summer on a pinch of sulphate of ammonia, feeding on the decayed turf, the humus from donkey's years of sheep manure, and that winter quality sprouts like that paid their way.

It seemed to me that this year marked in our village a pre-war ploughing up campaign, as Mr Nicklin ploughed the field called the Seeds and grew a terrific crop of British Lion peas.

CHAPTER TWENTY-ONE

In the Sweat of Thy Face

God said unto Adam, 'in the sweat of thy face shalt thou eat bread', and a long time ago, when I saw the land in my teens, this prediction seemed so true. Men worked in the '20s and '30s as their fathers had done. Seeing men going home at night scuffing their hob-nailed boots, tired out with hard labour, was real to me. It was as if there was something extremely virtuous in an aching back and sore feet. The fact was that if someone of my generation had the pluck to suggest an easier way of doing a job, he would be frowned on as a shuffler; someone who was collar proud. 'Collar proud' is just an expression describing a Monday morning work-shy horse who jibbed when the check lining of the collar tightened on his shoulders, shoulders that had been free from work on Sunday.

How it all comes back, the sowing of artificial [fertiliser]. Dad and Mr Bailey insisted that the sprouts, as soon as the plants had taken root, had a ration of sulphate of ammonia or nitrate of soda. This salt-like substance was carried up and down the sprout rows in buckets. A pinch of about a tablespoonful to be placed about an inch off the plant's stem. It mustn't touch it because it would burn up the plant. It mustn't be two or three inches away, because the so-called 'articificial' would not work and reach the roots of the plant.

This all seems so trivial to so many folk, but it wasn't to us. To get the stuff where it was wanted meant bending the back at every plant until the right hand could touch the ground and release its measure of chemical. I never heard of slipped discs.

The idea had never been thought of, but after a day of up and down every yard, the spine numbed. The only relief, as the summer sun warmed us at bait time (lunch), was to take half an hour lying flat on the grassy headland.

Of course the planting of all the crops of the cabbage family was done by setting-pins or dibbers, so also were the runner beans. I remember telling George my back ached and he laughed and said that my back wasn't long enough to ache.

I will say that when I worked for Messrs Archer and Bailey and we got what was termed 'mowed up', that is to say behind with our work, they did improvise a bit. For instance, to dig seven acres of asparagus beds when the sprouts were fit to pick often put them on the spot. So Ralph and I ploughed the beds with a little Ransome plough and two horses. It wasn't such a tidy job as what was known as 'alleying out' with a two-tine or prong fork. This involved digging up between the rows or beds and putting one spit or forkful to the left and the next to the right to lax with the winter frosts.

It was no mean task for Ralph to plough the asparagus beds. Sometimes when the clay lay like slices of cheese, yellow cheese, we looked back and watched as it slid back into the furrow. Then we tackled the strawberry rows. This was easier as the ground was level and we wrapped the winter-brown plants with a blanket of soil leaving an open furrow up between the rows. I thought this to be better than digging because the furrows drained the water from the strawberry roots. Older men were dubious. Frank and I were pleased, for only the winter before we had been broken in to two-tine or prong digging. Mr Bailey bought us two new forks from Averills at Evesham, and showed us the way to alley out 'gras' as asparagus was called. The chisel points of Uncle George's fork shone like silver. Ours were new and blunt. It looked so easy as the men turned the sods over. Frank and I, stripped to the braces, puffed and blowed to try and keep up with Uncle George. Then I watched him, saw that his fork was cranked to suit his build, realised that Frank and I were digging deeper than the rest. After midday dinner I took our forks to Tom

Higgins, the Sedgeberrow blacksmith. He smiled as he put them in the fire and bent the red-hot metal on his anvil. Back at work we found that Tom had taken some of the backache out of gras alleying.

Earlier I mentioned the ploughing of Quar Hill and how it grew sprouts. To me this was a turning point in the working of the land. You see, it was the accepted thing, a practice no one questioned, that Ralph mowed the brookside Hams first. The milking cows grazed Tun Flun, the horses Boss Close and Shepherd Tidmarsh lambed his ewes in Church Close. All permanent pasture. It takes a lifetime to make a good permanent ley, the old men said. The same thing applied to the plough land. Finches Piece grew the mangolds. I suspect this was because when the muck was carted from the cattle yards, this was the nearest arable field. So every year in early winter, the muck heaps in Finches Piece stood in rows like brown pitched tents ready for the spreading. Then the field was ploughed before Christmas. Cabbages grew year after year along Beckfords Way. The chickweed, like green mats, was horse-hoed, hand-hoed and never grew less. Peas in Hempits, where the near-by ditch turned the twigs into stone, a marvel to me in those days. Here coltsfoot smothered the land and scarlet pimpernel and groundsel competed with the peas. When the peas were clear of weeds by man power and horse power, sprouts were planted between the rows. It was always the same pattern; the old order never seemed to change. But the sprouts on Quar Hill did grow despite the limestone rock.

I'm sure that lack of change of crops and stock on the land is just asking for disease. A sheep's biggest enemy is another sheep and land gets sheep-sick. And so in the 1930s liver fluke struck our flock and the glassy eye, the lumpy jaws of the ewes, were indications of an early grave. Shepherd Tidmarsh grieved about his ewes as if they were his own. Every morning that lambing season one, two, three and even four ewes lay stiff under the orchard trees. The old man was heart-broken. The tears were in his eyes as he fetched his Friday night wage packet. He blamed himself, such was the loyalty of the man.

The following year Mr Bailey and Dad bought a kynd [thriving] lot of bulling heifers from Ireland and put them to the bull. Rich, dark red Shorthorns, as matching a lot of twelve cattle as peas in a pod. Tom Whittle described them as the best bunch he'd seen for many a day. Even the shepherd approved of them. They were turned out with a Hereford Bull.

In the foddering time, November until late April, I did the rounds with Tom the cowman. We carted hay to the store beef cattle, threw mangolds from the muck cart, then over the hill to Kersoe and fed the in-calves from Ireland.

One morning we found a calf about the size of a hare dead under the hedge. The heifer stood alongside. Tom gasped. 'That's done it,' he said. I don't know why, just bad luck I thought. The words Tom used to Dad when we arrived back in the yard were, 'One of the ayfers [heifers] has cast her calf.' They looked downcast, master and man, and said, 'It looks like a contagious abortion.' It was. We found another the next day, then another, and ten out of twelve all had dead calves after a six-month or so pregnancy.

The heifers gave about enough milk to rear one calf each, and I took them with Tom to Paris Barn where I reared the calves bought from Gloucester.

So with prices low and no answer to many diseases, the words of Goldsmith, 'ill fares the land', were true.

*   *   *

For three or four years before 1939, I read more and more about the power Hitler was gaining in Europe. It seemed like Napoleon all over again as his empire grew wider.

It has been a well-known saying that to make a politician Minister of Agriculture between the wars would be as far as he would ever get in that elite company who rule us. Our MP, W.S. Morrison, an able barrister, was appointed to try and put farming back on its feet.

Or was he appointed for that reason? He was certainly in Dad's opinion (and what Dad thought, I thought) a man for the time. With the threat of war the land could not be neglected. It had been neglected. Mr Morrison knew how poor and unproductive our pastures were. He introduced a subsidy on lime and basic slag. The acid land grew more grass as farmers took advantage of cheap lime. The basic slag put the clover back into the pastures.

The other thing our new minister did was to give a subsidy on beef cattle to encourage more home production. Thousands of acres of grassland hadn't had any fertiliser for years. The result was better crops or hay when the lime and slag was sown.

As I had been horse-raking one of our green grounds, as we called grassland, the crop was twice as much as the year before because of the dressing of basic slag. I came in saddle-sore after riding on the iron seat of the horse-rake one July evening. The wireless blared as Hitler gave one of his famous sabre-rattling speeches. No, I didn't understand German, but it was so easy to tell the mood of his listeners. I suppose he spoke of his ambition for Europe and I gather that our unemployment figures went down as a feeble effort was made to re-arm the country.

But what was the effect as I saw it?

The shepherd remembered more than one war and, as the scrap-iron Jacks came round the farm buying up the scrap implements, he said to me, 'That's a bad omen.' I wondered why, until he explained that before a war scrap iron was wanted for munitions. Puzzling days they were when the trouble in Abyssinia and Spain filled the front page of the *Daily Express*. Lord Beaverbrook had pleaded for years for Empire Free Trade. I think he was right. Despite what our minister of agriculture had done, the farmers were dissatisfied. Corn prices were still low.

One Saturday, after a morning buying calves on Gloucester Market, Dad and I went to hear Mr Morrison who had been invited to speak at the county National Farmers' Union, a meeting I'll never forget. Scores of farmers had their questions ready. After Mr Morrison's speech, the farmers had the opportunity to ask him what he proposed to do about low prices, gluts, etc. Here for the first time in my life it came home to me how careful one had to be in the construction of a question to a barrister, especially a Scot.

'Why import meat from the Empire when we can't sell our own fat stock?' one farmer asked. The minister pondered, pursed his lips. He looked dignified with his bushy eyebrows and his greying hair.

'You see, sir,' he said, 'we have trade agreements and in an emergency these could be amended, an emergency such as we find ourselves in today.' We thought for a moment he was going to put a damper on imports, but no, he came in with his important statement of fact which he kept until last. His magnificent Scots accent was more apparent as his voice raised. 'This is not the time to use the big stick on our Empire.' He knew something which we liked to dismiss from our minds; the imminence of total war on the horizon. Another question was about the price of lambs. I remember that Dad had bought in as unsold lambs at a pound apiece at Beckford Market that August. The Gloucestershire farmer in his long and wordy question included the remark that there had been a heavy fall of lambs that year.

'Surely, sir,' Mr Morrison came back with his prompt reply. 'Surely, sir, you are not going to blame me for a prolific lambing season.' The farmers laughed. He had won them over. What more could be said?

It seemed to me in those pre-war years that the minister of agriculture was a kind of scapegoat. Powers of compulsion on farmers had not yet come. His hands were tied by trade agreements, but as a go-between poised delicately twixt the Government and the farmers, W.S. Morrison did a good job.

Did it ever occur to you that these very grasslands, pastures improved through lime and slag when they were ploughed during the war, produced the grain and other crops which helped to save the country from starvation? That improved turf was an insurance; money in the bank waiting for the day when the great ploughing-up campaign produced crops that even surprised the experts.

Wages went up a few shillings a week. Army depots dug their foundations into farming land. The BBC bought Wood Norton to evacuate to in case of air raids. First-aid classes started in the village and Shepherd Tidmarsh said to me one day, 'Did you yer what Hitler bin saying, it's in this morning's paper? Thurs gwain to be another bust up afore long. I saw the scrap-iron Jacks round isterday.'

CHAPTER TWENTY-TWO

The Second-class Citizens

In the years just before the war, it seemed to me that the workers on the land were looked upon as still having the old image of country yokels. Swede gnawers, a little bit lacking.

This fallacy has been exposed by men like A.G. Street who knew so well that men who could plough, pitch hay and sheaves, layer hedges, shear sheep, milk cows, were far removed from the oafs which they were thought to be by so many who could turn a spanner in a car factory. Craftsmen of the highest order, they were underrated and underpaid.

You know, it took a lot of talking by the old Wages Board to raise the wage from thirty shillings to thirty-six shillings per fifty-hour week. The men were fairly satisfied, but what did rile them was that every time the wages rose slightly, the council roadmen, who mowed the verges, swept the road, were awarded a few shillings more than the farm worker. The farm worker had Good Friday off, while the roadman had both Good Friday and Easter Monday.

The local councils in this way did a lot to upset the farm worker. No, he didn't really care what the car workers earned in Birmingham, but the thought that the man over the hedge whose job was less exacting than his got an extra few shillings a week was a sore point.

Being right on the boundary between Worcestershire and Gloucestershire created another problem, as one county worked fifty-two hours for the same money as fifty hours worked in the other county.

The week's holiday with pay came not long before the
Second World War and up until then the only paid holidays
were Christmas Day and Good Friday.

There was, however, a will to work among the men of the
land. In our village this was fostered, I'm sure, by the fact that
the employers, 'the men as pays', as they were known, took
their coats off and worked with the men.

Mr Bailey, who died in 1936, had brought with him from
Evesham a code, a pattern, which just had to be followed by
the others. He carried neither tape measure nor pocket book,
but knew instinctively whether a job was being done properly
or not. These men of the old school of tillers of the soil worked
by what was known as 'scowl of brow'; a term which simply
meant experience, trial and error. And so I saw the men work
with a will.

Then the Government started building army camps. They
robbed the land of many good men. One camp planned at
Ashchurch dug its foundations into a good farm. The contractors offered labourers one and fivepence half-penny an hour.
What was a farm worker to do if he was getting ninepence an
hour? This was the beginning of the first exodus from our
village.

I remember Dad stood quite cool in our back yard that
Friday night when about five of our best men gave in their
notice.

These were men who weren't frightened of a day's work.
They started at Ashchurch digging the foundations.

The difference in attitude between the contractor, a man
who is never seen, and the working farmer is astounding.

George, who had worked hard for Dad since a boy, dug a
hole at Ashchurch easily by lunch time. He asked the foreman
what to do after lunch. 'Stand in there till knocking-off time,'
came the reply. I'm sure George would not be pleased about
that. He would want to get on with the job.

You see, the rot had set in. Set in by bad Government
policy. Policy where a foreman, who employed twenty men,
got more wages than one who did the same work with ten.

Then the contractors worked on a costs-plus basis. The more the building of the army camp cost, the more profit the contractors got.

How alien a system to country folk.

It's fair comment that the camps were needed urgently, but it's doubtful if this way of working made for an earlier completion. I thought it crooked, but then I'd been schooled by Archer and Bailey.

CHAPTER TWENTY-THREE

The Shepherd's Crook is Laid Aside

When old age catches up with a man, one part of the human frame gives way. I suppose in a way we are made like an engine. We wear away. Someone once said that the miracle of life is that 'A harp with a thousand strings should keep in tune so long'.

Shepherd Tidmarsh's legs gave way after a lifetime of trudging over first of all the Cotswold limestone, then the Vale clay.

A shepherd with a good dog walks miles over and over the same ground.

Shepherd Tidmarsh knew almost every stick and stone this side of Bredon. 'Never let yer ewes hear the church bells two weeks running from the same fields,' he often told me. We have read about the nomadic tribes and how they moved their flocks. The shepherd's theory of moving his ewes from field to field could not always be practised, but he moved them to pastures new when he could.

Then his legs gave way. I went to see him and he said in his usual humorous way, 'Fred bwoy, I was born too soon, but I be still all right up the top end.' I agreed that his brain was as active and alert as ever. His memory was good, but I could see that from now on he would be unable to cope with the sheep.

His advice, however, would be valuable. So he sat in his

chair, smoked his shag tobacco, while his dog retired with him.

It was a hot August Friday, just before Munich, when the shepherd left. Tom Whittle was looking after the cattle at Kersoe. One hundred and twenty Kerry ewes were up in the meadows. Tom came to our door on the Saturday. 'Master,' he said to Dad. 'I reckon the yows at Kersa got some company. Maggots!'

Dad said. 'We'll come up in the morning.' 'We' meaning Tom, Dad and me.

Walking back into the house that sultry August night, the mizzling rain came down Bredon Hill like spray. 'Muggy puthery hot,' Dad said it was, and he sighed as he added, 'It looks like a busy day among the sheep tomorrow. Your Collie puppy, Skipper, will be handy to get the ewes in a pen.' Skipper's coming along nicely now, I thought.

Dad sat in the wing chair and supped his bread and milk supper, blowing the first spoonful, then he turned to me and said, 'I wish the old shepherd had knocked off sooner. He kept going until he couldn't get round properly.'

'He's told me a lot,' I said to Dad, 'About sheep.'

'Right,' Dad said, 'you take over the ewes when we have put them straight, and Tom Whittle can keep an eye on you until you can manage.'

'Seems a long while ago since Ralph fetched his furniture on the waggon from the Duke's place. You was but twelve months old, the war was on. Now it looks like we shall have another war soon.' Dad replied.

That Sunday morning, I'll never forget. The overnight rain had stopped and the sun shone, drying the steaming hot fleeces on the ewes' backs. We went in Dad's car with my puppy and Tom Whittle took his cattle dog. I suppose it was about nine in the morning. As we approached the gate, Tom shouted, 'Yonder look, Master,' at a ewe gnashing her teeth as she tried in vain to bite what Izaak Walton called 'gentiles' from her rump. 'Another anant [next to her] looks to have maggots under her belly.' I stood and listened. Listened to the wealth of experience which came from the lips of Tom and Dad.

'See how her twitches, Master, that's the grub from the blue assed fly to be sure.'

'Oh, Lor,' Dad said as he mopped his brow, 'we shall be here all day and that won't be the end of this mess. Get round um with the dogs, Fred,' he said to me, and we drove them to the hurdled pen in the shade of the wych elms, down at the bottom of Big Holbrook in what was known as the Slingit.

With the crook I reversed one ewe after another to my elders who clipped away the soiled wool, poured on the Jeyes Fluid and scraped the fat maggots from live mutton with a penny.

The fly blows, or unhatched maggots, clung to the sheep's wool like saffron-coloured bran.

All day long we clipped and trimmed and dressed the sheep. Dressed the raw wounds with Stockholm Tar and Green Oils. It was a messy job.

One ewe had run against the knife of a mowing machine and gashed her side just in front of her hip. She was in a sorry state, as the fly's eggs had hatched to maggots and they moved on the flesh digging deep into her loin.

'What do you think about her, Tom?' Dad said.

Tom looked puzzled for a minute, then said, 'Can we take her down home, put her in the cool calf pen anant the bull pen?' We carried her to the boot of the car and roped her in.

Down in the calf pen after dinner, we washed her wound with soap and water. We killed all the maggots and sheared her for the second time that summer.

'Nasty place. How's it going to heal, Master?' Tom said. 'Never seen one so bad.'

Dad turned to me, sending me down to get the shepherd's advice. At Honeysuckle Cottage, Alf Tidmarsh sat in his wooden armchair, his collie dog lay at his feet.

'Come in, Fred bwoy, I bin thinking all the morning about how the ewes are this muggy weather. I only wish that it was possible for me to help. You've had some maggots, I'll warrant, or my name unt Alf Tidmarsh.'

'Coo!' I said. 'It's turned my stomach this morning, but we've won all except a ewe that has cut herself.'

'Be the varmints [maggots] got in dip?' he asked.

'Yes, and left a nasty hole, big enough to put my fist in.'

The old man lit his pipe while his wife poured me a cup of tea. He puffed and thought, then puffed the smoke from his Red Bell Shag until the room was full of smoke.

'Now listen carefully to what I'm gwain to tell ya.' I listened. 'Now tell yer father to get some fresh wood ashes and fill that hole in the ewe's loin. Make sure first of all there's no maggots left. You got that, have ya?' and I nodded. 'Now get the wool from round the wound and pull it across, tying it like a bandage.'

'But, Shepherd, we've sheared her.'

'Wuh, wuh, wuh,' he chuckled. 'That makes twice this summer. I had her pelt off in the end of May. Get a piece of clean cloth and tie round her belly with binder twine, that ull keep the ashes in place.' I went to leave, he called me back. 'Yer a minute,' he said, 'just let me know how her goes on, ull ya.'

Back in the calf pen I told the shepherd's tale. We followed his advice about the ashes, and Tom said, 'I'll be dalled if the old man a picked up a feow maxims about sheep since he left the Cotswolds.' On the cool brick floor the ewe got well again. 'Dried up as clean as a smelt,' Tom said.

It seemed odd that, after years of the shepherd managing the flock he was replaced by Tom and me part-time with the ewes, while Ralph looked after the lambs on the grass of the Far Ham.

Ralph, the carter, had no dog so he hurdled them up every morning, cracking his ploughman's whip like a .22 rifle, but as the lambs fattened and were sold, Ralph's shepherding came to an end and I have a feeling he was glad.

'Never cared for ship,' he said, 'allus boring through the hedges. They beunt like hosses, satisfied with the grass. Seems to me,' he said, 'that t'other side of the fence is where they aims to get.'

In September Dad bought two Ryland rams from Gloucester and Tom and I divided the ewes into two lots of fifty;

the older ewes went to market. So with their briskets raddled with red like waistcoats, the 'husband ship', as Tom called them, had fifty mates apiece. It reminded me of Thomas Hardy's raddle man as I plastered the paste on the rams every other morning and gave the ram a few beans to keep his strength up.

The red marks on the ewes' backs told me the ones he had served.

It always struck me how groomed and flat-backed the rams were presented for sale in the market and how different they looked by Christmas when the serving of the ewes and the winter weather had taken the bloom from their backs.

One Saturday Dad went to Gloucester Market and bought a dozen sandy-faced Welsh Radnor type of ewes. Tidy they looked to me, but they were the only ewes the ram left unmarked. They lay quiet with the flock all the winter. February came and they nibbled the ivy from the hedge bottoms and, where the early grass grew, they got out to it. They climbed the churchyard wall like cats, causing me more trouble than all the other sheep. They lambed early. They must have been in lamb when they came. Some lambed on the summit of Bredon, others by the brook. Those Welsh ewes worried me every night they were out until we sold them.

The other ewes lambed without much trouble. Dad helped if they were difficult and I moved them around the farm and, being young, could take them to pastures where the old shepherd had not been able to graze them.

In those days, before lamb dysentery could be prevented by either vaccine or serum, there was little one could do when it occurred. I lost quite a few good lambs through this nasty disease. It was disheartening, like that time the shepherd had lost ewes through liver fluke.

Tailing time came around about Easter. That's when a shepherd counts his crop.

Tom was dubious about tailing and castrating, as he had only castrated pigs. The shepherd promised to come and show us, but he just couldn't come to the yard and the lambs were getting big. Dad said to Tom, 'You have a go, but leave the biggest lambs' tails on, they seem too big now.'

I held the lambs and Tom sharpened the bone-handled shut knife, which once belonged to Aaron Allen, the squire's shepherd. We left the biggest lambs' tails on.

At Whitsun Harry Byrd, the Evesham Butcher, bought our best fat lambs at a shilling a pound. The ones with the tails fell behind and were not ready until later. So tailing a lamb does hasten its growth. The lambs were good and I felt proud when Dad said that I reared the best bunch they had had for several years. Just for one reason: I was young and able to move them around and tried not to let them hear the church bells ring twice while they were in the same field. I'd never claim to have the knowledge of Alf Tidmarsh, but when a man gets old and short of breath he is restricted in climbing hills. Age is often a gradual process unnoticed until it catches up in the end.

I met many conscientious men on the land when I was young, but never one who would measure up to Alf Tidmarsh.

On Sunday nights after Chapel, I visited the shepherd. We lived again seventy years among the sheep. He told me how he hurdled Cotswold tegs [year-old lambs] on turnips. 'Tegs like donkeys,' he said, 'they stood as high as the hurdles. Mind tha, Fred,' he always added, 'They was wonderful quiet, different from them hurdle jumpers yer father bought during the war.'

'What sort were they, Shepherd?' I said.

'Oi, Cheviots,' then he chuckled, twinkled his eye, looked at me, then at his wife. 'Shall I tell him, Missus?' he said. ''Cause they could run that fast the flies couldn't catch um. Oh no, no maggots on them, nor on that Western ram our neighbours had, he got out you know.'

'Got out where?' I said.

'Oi, among our yows and tupped um early.' He laughed again. 'Bald as a coot he was, no wool on his back and he stunck like a billy goat. Ah,' he sighed, 'when you bin on this earth nigh on eighty years, you've sin some fourpenny cut.'

'Tell me about the duke and the golden gates, Shepherd,' I ventured.

'Bless the bwoy, you don't want to stop yer all night! Just fetch me a glass of beetroot wine and bring Fred some herb beer.' The beetroot-wine was clear as claret in the glass and the old man smacked his lips and wiped his walrus moustache on his red spotted handkerchief.

'The duke, you said. Well, they called me Shepherd there but we hadn't got many sheep, 'twas more like a zoo.'

The man I was talking to had done so much in his life, nothing he said would have surprised me. From butchering sheep to doctoring cats. Living on boiled swedes as a boy and driving the bullocks at plough. I remembered it all, and how the plough-boys caught the bree flies and put them by the bullocks' ears so they ran away with the plough. I just wanted to know about the duke; it seemed important to me to work for a duke. He told me his story of how his time was spent at Norton when the few sheep were looked after for the day. Apparently loads of wild animals came from all over the world to Evesham station to establish a zoo at Norton. The deer were thick in the woods and keepers reared hundreds of pheasants for the big shoots in the autumn. The duchess, he told me, was no ordinary lady. 'She made me help the keepers after a deer shoot to sit the dead stags on the lawn in front of the drawing room life-like and looking through the windows.'

'What for?' I said. The shepherd held the Sunday paper in his hand and pointed with his finger.

'See the pictures in thur,' he said, 'well, they be only photographs. Her was an artist, her liked drawing stags.'

'Oh I see, but who came to the shoots?'

He gave me the answer, 'Royalty.'

Then I heard how the kings of Europe all came to shoot pheasants and deer. The old man laughed when he related how one winter the pheasants fell in such numbers to the gun that Norton got short of birds. That was the year, he said, when it was either the king of Spain or Portugal who took on a bet with the duke that he could not get two dead birds falling in the air together, and the king had three on the way to earth as he shot in a deep valley between the woods, where the pheasants flew over high, looking no bigger than starlings.

'What happened when you got short of birds?' I asked.

The old man laughed as he relived it all again. 'A load came to Evesham Station in crates from abroad.'

The conversation stopped a minute or two while he and his wife laughed until the tears rolled down their cheeks. I was glad to see them amused and asked if they were the wrong sort of birds.

'They were pheasants all right,' the shepherd said, and he told me how the keepers loosed them from their crates into the woods several days before the big shoot; well, it should have been a big shoot.

'Out with it, Alf, you might as well tell Fred your secret,' Mrs Tidmarsh said.

'Well, it was like this,' he said. 'I was helping the beaters to flush the game in front of the guns that day, and the pheasants wouldn't fly. They just squat on the ground among the blackberry bushes.'

'Strange cover for them in the English woods,' I said.

'No, 'twasn't that, it was the elastic bands. You see, when they come from abroad in the crates, their wings were strapped down with elastic bands so that they couldn't fly, and the keepers forgot to take the elastic bands off when they released them from the crates.'

I asked the shepherd, who now looked quite solemn, what became of the pheasants and he told me that they couldn't rise to perch in the trees and the foxes killed them. The gentry had a bad day, only shooting about a dozen brace of the native birds. 'That was a rum un, wasn't it,' he added.

When I asked for more about what happened behind the golden gates, he told me how a man came on purpose to put a coat of gold on the gates when they got dull, and how he, the shepherd, was sort of lackey to the duke, riding to Evesham on a hunter every day to collect shopping and do errands. 'I allus called at the Jolly Gardener for half a pint and the horse had a lump of sugar,' he said. One morning the duke rode to town and couldn't get the horse past the Jolly Gardener until the barmaid gave the horse a lump of sugar. The duke was amused, knowing full well that his young shepherd called regularly for a drink as well.

These Sunday visits to Honeysuckle Cottage were memorable. They showed to me what Alf Tidmarsh had contributed to the life of the Vale and the Hills, how he had been content with so little.

The 1939 war started in the following September and the shepherd's health got worse. He told me where to pick the agrimony flowers to make tea. 'It's me water,' he said. I took bunches of the primrose-coloured spikes, fragrant flowers which had probably done him good in earlier years.

One Monday morning I passed the window. The curtains were drawn and, over the garden hedge, Mrs Tidmarsh whispered, 'Alf's dead, went off in his sleep.'

Four of his fellow landworkers carried him to his last resting place. I stood that hot afternoon on the right-hand side of the font as they brought the old warrior home. 'Change and decay in all around I see,' we sang and my tears trickled into the hymn book. The vicar said some comforting words and, as the webbing lowered him into the clay, I thought, 'That's the shepherd's body but his humour, his concert songs and his memory will live as long as I walk Ashton village.'

CHAPTER TWENTY-FOUR

The Last Days of the Old Ashton

Old men with whom I'd worked, eaten my ten o'clock bait, sat by in Chapel, on the cricket field, at socials, parochial teas and so on, told me two things which were as real to me as if I had experienced them. First of all, that the winters were not so cold or the summers so hot and haymaking days so long as before the first Great War. Secondly they impressed upon me that 'Things were never the same again after the war'.

This is true and no one could argue that the first decade of this century had more than its share of hard winters and hot summers, or that things are ever the same after a war.

So I pictured these men with sacking tied on the soles of their hob-nailed boots walking on the icy roads.

I saw the horses with chisel frost nails in their shoes pulling waggons up our steep village street. Dad talked of men hawking boxes of herrings around the villages to earn a living, or more true to say, buy bread.

But Tom Whittle had told me of a summer one year when they drew their harvest money on August Monday. All was gathered in. It was no doubt an age of extremes. Men cut willow branches off the summer trees to feed the cattle. The summer grass was burnt up like a desert. Yes, I believe this. It's been proved that by and large old men speak the truth as they look back over life.

The fact that great changes took place after the 1914–18 war, one has to accept also. Village boys had travelled on the Continent, the Middle East and farther afield. They came back with a broader view of the world. And so when the war clouds were again on our horizon and our village culture, however poor, was threatened, a gloom gathered after Munich. You may ask why. The answer is quite simple. No born country-man ever trusted politicians. The town people were probably the same, but there is a marked difference in outlook.

It was obvious to us all that after Munich the trade depression was eased. Prices were better as men earned a bit more on munition work.

I saw a few more cars come to the village. Farm workers' wages went up slightly and the odd one or two could run a BSA 250 motor-bike. But beneath it all was a suspicion that soon our village, with every other one, would be directed what to do.

The siren practised at Evesham. Old soldiers of the First War talked of mustard gas.

A true countryman of 1938 was fairly happy with his lot, his measure, like a bushel measure of independence. If you say how parochial, or even selfish, this seems, you've never lived in a village in the '20s and '30s. On paper the farm worker was a poor peasant, but in his heart, in his cottage and garden he was rich. Riches which cannot be bought with gold.

Some may smile at this 'Every man sitting under his own fig tree' story, but what value can be put on independence? In earlier chapters, I've stressed Dad's dread of ever being completely ruled from Whitehall. The villagers had not forgotten his fight for the right to work an allotment, his right to shoot a rabbit on his allotment. At last men on the land were enjoying a few day's holiday. Holidays even if they were only spent with relatives in a Welsh mining valley or in the Black Country. It seemed that if only this respite from the Depression of the early '30s could have developed into a lasting prosperity for everyone, how good that would have been. But thirty-six miles from Birmingham, we knew that the work which had been found for the unemployed was in the main the manufacture of machines to preserve our very existence. The need for khaki, lorries and gun carriers.

Our local council planned more council houses in Finches Piece, houses to get their water supply from Paris on the hill.

The last crop of mangolds was cleared. The bury blocked the view from the Beckford Road like an earthwork. But only Red Chiefs and Yellow Globes, varieties of mangold wurzel, lay beneath the asparagus bower or fern which covered them from the frost and kept the soil off the root, which by some miracle of nature was rich in sugar after Christmas. The soil-covered bury had straw chimneys; wisps of straw to let the moist air escape, or any heat which formed in the heap of roots.

Finches Piece lay a barren three acres and a half, barren behind the bury and alongside the old orchard.

Young couples in the village, hungry for houses, grew impatient. Dad rang the council surveyor. I heard his voice in our kitchen. It was something like this: 'Hello, can I speak to Mr Atkinson please? Ah, Archer speaking. Could you send a load or two of bricks to Finches Piece or even a few scaffold poles? Why? Well, the people keep coming here and asking me when a start will be made on the houses.'

I gathered that Dad, a council member for the village, had another problem here. The water supply was sure but bricks were going to build Ashchurch Camp. Finches Piece waited. Mr Atkinson sent a load of scaffold poles.

It had seemed an age since the council had bought Finches Piece, three and a half acres, or thereabouts, off Dad for three hundred and fifty pounds! It must have been soon after Mr Bailey died in 1936.

His death had been quite a blow to me. He faded from a strong man in three months, then slipped away. I never went in Finches Piece without thinking of him. Remembering the afternoon when he cut a road around the wheat with a bagging hook and pick thank, a road for Ralph and the binder to cut the corn. He showed me that day how to bind a sheaf with a straw bond. Then there was the unexciting squitch [or couch grass], digging in the field corner under the withy tree at the bottom. Here Mr Bailey, stripped to the braces, dug up sods of earth and forked the squitch on to the top. I picked up the elver-like white roots, while Mr Bailey told me not to miss a piece which had two ends. It all went in the bucket. A most boring job it would have been had not my partner that day kept me continually amused with his tales of his boyhood and youth, his exploits with his gun. His gun seemed a part of him, and that October afternoon it lay loaded on his jacket for, if a stray pheasant had come to feed off the windfall apples in the adjoining orchard, I would have been sent in a wide arc to flush the bird towards him, and my bet would have been on the gun, and a Sunday dinner of pheasant for Mr Bailey.

But Finches Piece had been surveyed by 1939 and the scaffold poles lay under the hedge. I recall that last summer of peace, and how the Purple Egg plums hung on the trees like onions on the Brittany hawkers' cycle handlebars. The pickers were way behind and the sun turned the last few rows into growing prunes.

I went most evenings in late August to Stratford-on-Avon Canners and helped my brother Tom to unload his lorry.

Men were painting white lines up the middle of the main road. If the lorry lights were dimmed, the lines would at least show the middle of the road.

As the ultimatum to Germany ended at eleven a.m. the following Sunday, I sat with Dad and listened to Neville Chamberlain's broadcast to the nation. So once more we were at war.

The cattle got out of the Middle Dewrest in the afternoon. I got them back with Skipper, my dog, and mended the fence into the old meadow. The drinking pool was muddy so I shovelled it out. Walking back across the field I saw the white blossoms had turned brown. The clover grew thick after the basic slag fertiliser. I thought of Mr Morrison's wisdom when he subsidised slag. The fact that each root of clover was a pocket of stored nitrogen made me take a second look at the brookside meadow.

Little did I think that soon that nitrogen would be cashed as the plough broke swards of meadow which had grown nothing but grass since the Crimea, and now the green fields would be golden with wheat once more.

And so ended an age in Ashton. The lights were dimmed in the cottages. The scaffold poles were fetched away from Finches Piece.

Life would never be the same again, but once more the produce of the land was vital. Wheat would grow instead of houses in Finches Piece.